T0325277

Founded in 1972, the Institute for Research on Public Policy is an independent, national, nonprofit organization. Its mission is to improve public policy in Canada by promoting and contributing to a policy process that is more broadly based, informed and effective.

In pursuit of this mission, the IRPP

- identifies significant public policy questions that will confront Canada in the longer term future and undertakes independent research into these questions;

- promotes wide dissemination of key results from its own and other research activities;

- encourages non-partisan discussion and criticism of public policy issues in a manner which elicits broad participation from all sectors and regions of Canadian society and links research with processes of social learning and policy formation.

The IRPP's independence is assured by an endowment fund, to which federal and provincial governments and the private sector have contributed.

Créé en 1972, l'Institut de recherche en politiques publiques est un organisme national et indépendant à but non lucratif.

L'IRPP a pour mission de favoriser le développement de la pensée politique au Canada par son appui et son apport à un processus élargi, plus éclairé et plus efficace d'élaboration et d'expression des politiques publiques.

Dans le cadre de cette mission, l'IRPP a pour mandat :

- d'identifier les questions politiques auxquelles le Canada sera confronté dans l'avenir et d'entreprendre des recherches indépendantes à leur sujet;

- de favoriser une large diffusion des résultats les plus importants de ses propres recherches et de celles des autres sur ces questions;

- de promouvoir une analyse et une discussion objectives des questions politiques de manière à faire participer activement au débat public tous les secteurs de la société canadienne et toutes les régions du pays, et à rattacher la recherche à l'évolution sociale et à l'élaboration de politiques.

L'indépendance de l'IRPP est assurée par les revenus d'un fonds de dotation auquel ont souscrit les gouvernements fédéral et provinciaux, ainsi que le secteur privé.

INSTITUTE FOR RESEARCH ON PUBLIC POLICY

INSTITUT DE RECHERCHE EN POLITIQUES PUBLIQUES

andrew sancton

governing canada's city-regions:

adapting form to function

series edited by
france st-hilaire

Printed in Canada
Second Printing August 1995

Bibliothèque nationale du Québec
Dépôt légal 1994

Canadian Cataloguing in Publication Data

Sancton, Andrew, 1948-
Governing Canada's city-regions : adapting form to function

(Monograph series on cities ; 2)

Includes bibliographical references.

ISBN 0-88645-156-6

1. Metropolitan government—Canada.
I. Institute for Research on Public Policy. II. Title. III. Series

JS1708.S25 1994   352'.0094'0971   C94-900573-8

Marye Bos
Executive Director, IRPP

Copy Editor
Mathew Horsman

Design and Production
Ric Little and Barbara Rosenstein, Studio Duotone inc.

Cover Illustration
Tanya Johnston, Studio Duotone inc.

Published by
The Institute for Research on Public Policy (IRPP)
L'Institut de recherche en politiques publiques
1470 Peel Street, Suite 200
Montreal, Quebec H3A 1T1

Distributed by
Renouf Publishing Co. Ltd.
1294 Algoma Road
Ottawa, Ontario K1B 3W8
For orders, call 613-741-4333

Contents

List of Tables and Maps

Foreword

City-regions are key transmission points in the global economy. They are home to skilled labour, extensive communications and transportation networks and the most supple and innovative of firms. Yet the importance of city-regions, and the extent of their role in driving the economy, is poorly recognized in Canada. Local government structures are often unwieldy; tax and transfer systems are out of sync with the form and function of modern city-region economies; provincial and federal economic development policy, with its traditional emphasis on sector-specific approaches and inter-regional equalization, does not adequately address the particular needs of cities.

In what way has the role of city-regions evolved over the past twenty years of structural economic change? How should government policy be altered to reflect the importance of city-regions in the new economy? How should the division of power among federal, provincial and local governments be reordered to better reflect current realities? Must we reform local-government financing, to provide a better match between local service delivery and local financing capability?

These are some of the questions the contributors to the IRPP's monograph series on City-Regions seek to answer. In the first volume, published earlier this year, Professor William Coffey of the Université du Québec à Montréal described the evolution of a new "non-industrial" economy, and suggested that global restructuring is having a profound effect on Canada's metropolitan regions. In the present monograph, the second in our series, Andrew Sancton of the University of Western Ontario analyzes existing governmental structures in Canada's city-regions and recommends that reforms be implemented to reflect new economic and spatial realities. In *Governing Canada's City-Regions: Adapting Form to Function*, he calls for the creation of new institutional frameworks in which the interests of entire city-regions can be served.

Soon to be published is a multi-author study of the main issues faced by local governments in the current fiscal environment. The topics include: the realignment of provincial and local responsibilities; local revenue diversification; user fees and the pricing of municipal services; and new approaches to infrastructure provision. Other topics in the City-Region series, to be produced under the editorial direction of IRPP Senior Researcher France St-Hilaire, include the role of cities as economic gateways as well as a number of case studies focussing on the distinct concerns and issues facing Canada's largest city-regions.

The IRPP is extremely pleased to be bringing this excellent work to the attention of a wide audience. Governance issues are essential to improving the efficiency of municipalities in Canada: reforms in this area will go a long way toward creating institutional structures capable of responding to the needs of a changing economy. Finally, it should be noted that the opinions expressed in this study are the responsibility of the author and do not necessarily reflect the views of IRPP or its Board of Directors.

Monique Jérôme-Forget
President, IRPP

Editor's Introduction

The process of urban growth and development inevitably gives rise to new administrative requirements for managing existing growth, accommodating the demand for additional services and planning future development in and around a given metropolitan area. With few exceptions, the instrument of choice used in the past to cope with urban problems in Canada has been structural reform. The efforts of Canadian municipal reformers have been focussed primarily on dealing with "irrational" boundaries and avoiding fragmentation – generally through annexation, amalgamation and/or the implementation of two-tier systems of local government. Reformers invariably stress as justifications the need to capture economies of scale and the importance of being able to plan outward expansion. Underlying the traditional approaches to local governance in Canada is the basic assumption that the solution to most problems associated with urban development lies in devising and putting in place the "right" municipal structure.

One of the main arguments put forward by Andrew Sancton in this monograph is that we need to take a closer look both at the objectives pursued through municipal reform in Canada and the conventional means of achieving these objectives. The author questions, in particular, commonly held views concerning the need for and the benefits obtained from consolidation and the presumed accountability problems that are said to result from inter-municipal agreements and the establishment of special-purpose bodies. Sancton also deplores the absence of debate about some of the positive aspects of fragmentation.

Based on a comparative analysis of Canada's metropolitan governments, Professor Sancton evaluates existing institutional arrangements in various Canadian city-regions. He argues that the priority should be, above all, the provision of *efficient* and *effective* municipal government and it is from this standpoint that he undertakes his assessment. Generally, efficiency is assumed to be promoted through clear political accountability. This does appear to be the outcome in a number of Canadian cities with comprehensive single-tier municipal systems. However, as Sancton points out, it is important to realize that efficiency can also be derived from the discipline of the marketplace. Indeed, the presence of competing municipalities need not result in waste, duplication and overlap, as is often argued, but rather in choice, specialization and efficiency.

The author argues, furthermore, that the debate on urban problems and the types of solutions put forward become quite different when municipalities are viewed as "arrangers" rather than "producers" of services. The issue of appropriate borders becomes less central and functional alternatives to structural reform can be considered. The time may have come for such a change of perspective. First, it is not at all clear, given the pace and nature of urbanization in Canada, that any city-region can ever have in place, for any length of time, the optimal municipal structure. Secondly, as some critics point out in response to the latest proposal for new structures in the Greater Montreal region, municipal reform initiatives usually result in the establishment of increasingly complex and costly technocratic structures to enable the planning and management of growth over ever-expanding areas.

The cautious reaction to what could be interpreted as a three-tier system recently recommended for Montreal and the search for positively "non-structural" solutions to Toronto's current problems demonstrate not only the structural rigidities left over from past reforms but also the fact that the structural reform reflex is no longer as automatic as it once was. Nonetheless, Montreal, Toronto and several other cities at the core of Canada's major city-regions must continue to find ways to deal with the growing social and economic interdependencies that exist among the various municipalities within their respective region. Sancton sees in the Greater Vancouver Regional District a model that may have merit in terms of adaptability and efficiency and one which, given a somewhat expanded role, could be very effective.

The present challenge for many Canadian cities is perhaps best represented in the mandate assigned in 1991 to the Task Force on Local Government in Nova Scotia – that is, to come up with an appropriate form of local government that reflects existing settlement patterns and balances the concepts of economic and service-delivery efficiency on the one hand with those of accountability and accessibility on the other. What this monograph suggests, however, is that old assumptions about structural reform need to be reexamined and that innovation is the order of the day.

France St-Hilaire
Series Editor

Introduction

Major Canadian cities such as Toronto, Montreal and Vancouver are not physically constrained by the boundaries of their central municipalities. Urban development stretches far beyond the city limits, often encompassing many additional municipalities, each of which has much the same legal status as the one at the centre. Such fragmentation has been the cause of considerable debate, numerous government commissions and occasional attempts at major structural consolidation. Conventional justifications for consolidation point to potential economies of scale, the need for equity in access to taxation revenues and the virtues of regional planning. In the changing economic and technological environment of the 1990s, these arguments are in desperate need of re-examination.

No longer can we attempt to solve public-sector problems by simply adding new and costly structures to what we already have. Nor can we assume that an increase in funds will be available to ease the transition from one set of structures to another. Indeed, the opposite is the case: fiscal downloading from federal and provincial governments inevitably means that local governments – whatever their structures – must learn to adapt to a net reduction in financial resources. At the same time, despite limited resources, local governments are increasingly held responsible not just for providing local services but also for generating economic growth and development.

Economic Development

Canadian municipalities have long been involved in economic boosterism. Attracting the attention of nineteenth-century railway promoters is perhaps the best historical example of such activity. In the past, municipalities have been relatively passive providers of subsidies and concessions. While these practices are now illegal in many parts of the country, demands on local officials from voters and businesses to promote stable employment and market opportunities are greater than ever. In short, there are growing expectations that local governments must develop realistic strategies to ensure the economic health of their respective communities. Past debates about appropriate structural arrangements for local government in urban areas have not taken such demands into account. In this monograph, I aim to help correct this omission by focussing on some of the possible linkages – both direct and indirect – between economic development and the structures of local government.

For the purposes of this project, local economic development is defined as any increase in real per-capita earned income within the defined locality, exclusive of tax payments to outside governments. It is important to note that there is no necessary causal link between actual local economic development and government policies explicitly aimed at promoting growth. Local economic development could take place despite rather than because of such government policies; or it could be the unintended consequence of seemingly unrelated government policies. In any event, this monograph is in no way meant to be an assessment of conventional economic-development policies such as the offering of tax incentives and subsidies or the building of research parks and convention centres. Indeed, an underlying theme is that the best structural arrangements for local economic *development* are simply those that are most likely to promote effective and efficient local *government.* Innovations in structural arrangements are required – but not because of any peculiar requirements emanating from the imperatives of local economic development.

Possible strategies for promoting local economic development are remarkably varied. Unless we know what kind of strategy is being attempted for a given city, it is impossible to specify the types of institutions that are most likely to be appropriate. For example, if a central component of the strategy were to lower property taxes on manufacturing facilities so as to attract new jobs from outside the province, a province might ensure that there were many municipalities in any given urban area and then allow each one to grant tax concessions (or "bonuses") to individual manufacturers. Alternatively, if the strategy featured an integrated, comprehensive, enforceable land-use plan so as to optimize the use of land and public infrastructure, then a single municipality for the whole area is probably what would be required.[1]

In the real world, economic-development policies are never designed in such simple, one-dimensional terms. That is why the ideal structural arrangements for municipal government in metropolitan areas fall somewhere between these two extremes. For the largest metropolitan areas, at least, there needs to be some element of diversity and competition among municipalities and there needs to be some authority capable of providing an overall perspective. We are therefore led inexorably toward some form of two-tier system.

The main object of this project is to assess various existing institutional arrangements in terms of their compatibility with the economic development of Canada's city-regions. This will be done by analyzing the advantages and disadvantages of four different kinds of local-government systems, bearing in mind that all of them are subject to high levels of provincial control and regulation.

City-Regions

For the purposes of this study, Canada's city-regions will generally be considered to be synonymous with what Statistics Canada calls "census metropolitan areas" (CMAs). CMAs comprise "a very large urban area, together with adjacent urban and rural areas which have a high degree of economic and social integration with that urban area."[2] To be classified as a CMA, a city must have an "urbanized core" with a population of at least 100,000. In the 1991 Census of Canada, there were 25 CMAs.

Four of the CMAs – Toronto, Hamilton, St. Catharines-Niagara and Oshawa – are contiguous. They form what is often called the Golden Horseshoe around the western end of Lake Ontario. There is much to be said for treating this entire area as one "city-region." Indeed, for provincial planning purposes, the Ontario government once designated an area even larger than this as the "Toronto-Centred Region."[3] Because of its complexity, there is bound to be a degree of arbitrariness however one defines the Toronto city-region. But there are at least two especially significant problems in treating each of the four Toronto-area CMAs as distinct entities. First, Oshawa, to the east of Toronto, is too obviously a satellite to be considered an entity on its own. If the concept of city-region is to mean anything, then Oshawa must be considered part of the Toronto city-region. The second problem is that, although there may be good reasons for treating Hamilton as a more distinct entity than Oshawa, its CMA, as defined by Statistics Canada, includes the City of Burlington, whose links are arguably as strong with Toronto as with Hamilton.

As already indicated, the Ontario government is all too aware of the kinds of issues described above, especially since it runs its own train service (GO Transit) linking both Hamilton and Oshawa to downtown Toronto and points in between. In 1988, the provincial government designated the boundaries of the Greater Toronto Area (GTA) for purposes of planning its own policies and approaches in the wider Toronto city-region.[4] Exactly what is involved in the GTA will be described in more detail in chapter 5. For current purposes, it is important to remember that, for the rest of this study, the Toronto, Hamilton and Oshawa CMAs will not be used. The Toronto city-region will be considered synonymous with the GTA. Since the GTA includes only part of the Hamilton CMA, Hamilton is not properly integrated into this study.

In the chapters that follow, each of the remaining 22 CMAs (and, of course, the GTA) will at least be mentioned and its system of municipal government categorized in one of four ways. Some city-regions (e.g., Halifax, Toronto, Montreal, Vancouver, St. Catharines-Niagara, London) will be discussed in more detail, either because of the intrinsic importance of the particular city or because of the distinct or representative characteristics of its municipal-government arrangements.

In chapter 1, we look at municipal structures and functions and at the method used in this monograph for categorizing the municipal governmental systems of the 23 city-regions. Each of chapters 2 through 5 is devoted to describing and analyzing one of the categories. We conclude with an outline of the three main lessons derived from the overall study.

Notes

1. For a discussion of these and related issues, see Paul Kantor and H.V. Savitch, "Can Politicians Bargain with Business? A Theoretical and Comparative Perspective on Urban Development," *Urban Affairs Quarterly*, Vol. 29, no. 2 (December 1993), pp. 230-55.

2. Statistics Canada, *A National Overview*, 1991 Census of Canada (Ottawa: Supply and Services Canada, 1992), Catalogue no. 93-301, p. 29.

3. Frances Frisken, "Planning and Servicing the Greater Toronto Area: The Interplay of Provincial and Municipal Interests," in Donald N. Rothblatt and Andrew Sancton (eds.), *Metropolitan Governance: American/Canadian Intergovernmental Perspectives* (Berkeley, CA: Institute of Governmental Studies Press, 1993), pp. 171-217.

4. Frisken, "Planning and Servicing," p. 161.

1

Municipal Structures and Functions

The Functional Capacity of Local Government

In any given city-region, the system of local government comprises two types of institutions. The first are municipalities. Their main distinguishing characteristic is that they are multi-purpose. They are responsible, with varying measures of autonomy, for a range of government functions, some of which seem relatively unrelated to one another (regulating taxis and maintaining parks, for example). The other institutions making up local government are special-purpose bodies. As their name implies, they are concerned only with one government function, or a set of closely related ones. Boards of education in most provinces are the best examples of relatively powerful and important local special-purpose bodies. All local governments – both municipalities and special-purpose bodies – are under the formal political control of locally elected representatives or of people appointed by such representatives.[1]

What local governments actually do – or can do – is obviously of prime importance in determining their relevance for economic development. A mere listing of official functions – land-use planning, sewage treatment, etc. – is not of much intrinsic use in determining their importance. This is because the capacity to use legal authority in relation to a particular function to bring about a desired policy objective is intimately related to two other important factors: the territory covered by the local government and the degree of autonomy it has in relation to other institutions with which it must work.

The territorial factor is relatively simple. Having responsibility for a government function without having suitable territorial jurisdiction dramatically reduces a local government's capacity for independent action. For example, a municipality's control over land-use planning might seem impressive – until one realizes that all the land within its territory is already developed and in use. The function could only really be effectively exercised if the territory is extended to take in undeveloped land.

The autonomy factor is much more difficult and has increasingly occupied the attention of political scientists specializing in urban government.[2] Whether zoning by-laws require provincial approval or whether municipalities can act independently to implement new kinds of local taxation are crucial questions. For example, what does it mean to say that municipalities control land-use planning when, as in Ontario, just about any such decision they might make can be appealed to a quasi-judicial provincial agency known as the Ontario Municipal Board?[3] Notwithstanding the fact that municipalities outside Ontario generally have more autonomy in land-use planning, there are no Canadian local governments that are politically autonomous in any meaningful sense. They have no constitutional protection whatever against provincial laws that change their structures, functions and financial resources without their consent. For many of their responsibilities, they are subject to detailed administrative control from a wide range of provincial ministries, especially if conditional grants are involved.

Efforts to compare levels of local-government autonomy in Canada by comparing functions or sources of revenue are doomed to failure. For example, Ontario municipalities seem much more reliant on provincial grants than Quebec municipalities. But this can be explained by the fact that Ontario municipalities are still involved in a part (General Welfare Assistance) of the income-maintenance system, for which they receive high levels of provincial funding. Which municipalities are more autonomous – the ones with the higher levels of own-source funding or the ones involved in more government functions?

Ontario municipalities share at least half their property-tax base with school boards. In Quebec, the school-board share is much smaller because levels of provincial grants to school boards are higher. If we look at aggregate data for all local governments, we find that in 1990 local-government own-source revenues in Quebec were 54 percent of total revenue, while in Ontario the equivalent figure was 62.7 percent.[4] But if school-board revenues were removed from these figures, the relative positions would be reversed. What are we to conclude? Only that aggregate data such as these can be highly misleading if used as a measure of relative municipal autonomy.

In the United States, there is much less state-government control over local government than there is provincial control in Canada. Yet many observers have noted that American municipal governments seem even less capable than their Canadian counterparts in dealing with the social problems of huge metropolitan areas. This seems to be the case even in cities with African-American mayors and local majorities apparently committed to bringing about some form of dramatic social change. The problem is not one of political will. The problem is that, if a central-city municipality raises taxes to finance new social programs, many taxpayers – especially relatively wealthy owners of homes and businesses – will leave, not necessarily to another city, but to a nearby suburban jurisdiction in the same metropolitan area, where the taxes might be lower and the services better. In such circumstances, central-city revenues are not raised and social problems remain unaddressed. In the absence of any revenue-sharing system whereby richer municipalities are forced to subsidize poorer ones, the apparent legal autonomy of American municipalities is often a cruel fiction. US central cities with thousands of homeless residents, a booming drug trade and collapsing infrastructure can take little satisfaction in so-called "Home Rule" charters. What they really need is sufficient financial assistance from federal and state governments to enable them to compete with suburban municipalities for new business investment and middle-class residents.[5]

For Americans, the possibility of a comprehensive federal policy on urban issues is still an issue for public debate.[6] Even after the implementation of the decentralizing "new federalism" by presidents Reagan and Bush, the federal financial and regulatory presence in American urban municipalities is far greater than in Canada. But the importance of American federal-government constraints on municipal autonomy pale in comparison to those imposed by the inter-municipal marketplace. The constraints deriving from the imperatives of inter-municipal competition in the US are at least as significant as any imposed in Canada by provincial governments and they are far more damaging to the quality of urban life.

Rather than attempting to increase their capacity to influence central-government activities within their own areas, many Canadian local political leaders seem anxious to detach, or disentangle, themselves from involvement with a wide range of provincial-government programs and policies.[7] The interest of municipal politicians in disentanglement is often inspired by their fear of fiscal "downloading" – the process by which higher levels of government attempt to improve their financial position by reducing unconditional grants to lower levels or by failing to increase conditional grants to match higher demand for particular services.[8] Municipal politicians rightly assume that less municipal reliance on provincial funds means a greater likelihood in the future of avoiding the adverse financial consequences of downloading. The danger of such an assumption, however, is that municipal leaders may resist involvement with provincially funded governmental functions that are of crucial importance to the well-being of their communities. In Ontario, municipal reluctance in the late 1970s to take on responsibility for allocating provincial funds to non-profit agencies delivering services to children is a prime example.[9]

If municipalities wish to retain their ability to influence public policy within their communities, they must simultaneously resist downloading and promote devolution. The two objectives need not be incompatible. In Ontario, the municipal effort to wrest control of subdivision approval from the Ministry of Municipal Affairs is a clear example of relatively costless devolution.[10] In Quebec, officials within the City of Montreal have aggressively promoted the view that the municipality can effectively achieve its objectives only if its functional responsibilities are extended.[11] For Montreal, fear of future downloading seems not to be a deterrent in its efforts to become more involved in social concerns. The reality elsewhere, however, is that provinces are still becoming more – rather than less – involved in government functions once considered purely local.[12] Growing provincial involvement in the disposal of solid waste is a prime example.

A possible explanation for increased provincial involvement in local-government issues is that current municipal structures are insufficiently comprehensive in both territory and function to handle the most significant issues facing Canada's city-regions. The implications of such an explanation will be addressed throughout the rest of this monograph. For now, the point need only be made that such a position is not new: it has been taken with varying degrees of success by structural reformers in Montreal and Toronto since at least the 1920s. Whether or not one believes that provinces will one day be willing to devolve significant authority to enlarged municipal structures inevitably affects one's position on the optimal form of local-government organization.

Much of what follows is based on the premise that extensive devolution of provincial authority to municipalities is not a realistic option.[13]

---

table 1
major functional responsibilities of canadian local governments

Public education – elementary and secondary
Policing
Fire protection
Animal control
Roads – traffic control, parking and street-lighting
Public transit
Water supply (and sometimes electricity, natural gas or telephones)
Sewage – collection and treatment
Solid waste – collection and disposal
Land-use planning and regulation
Building regulation
Economic development and promotion
Public libraries
Parks and recreation
Public cultural facilities – museums, concert halls, art galleries
Licensing of businesses
Emergency planning

Table 1 contains a list of the major functional responsibilities of Canadian local government. No such list can be totally comprehensive; nor can it take account of the peculiarities of particular provinces or the special arrangements for different cities even within the same province. Missing from the list are any functions relating to public health and to social services. In the smaller provinces, these are generally entirely under provincial control. In Quebec, the province dominates but is assisted by various local special-purpose bodies, such as regional health and social services councils, social service centres, and local community service centres.[14] All of these locally based state agencies have their own boards of directors. In Ontario, municipalities still retain some social-service and public-health functions, but their involvement is subject to constant review and debate, most recently as part of the effort to disentangle provincial and municipal responsibilities.

Of all the government functions listed in table 1, public education costs the most money. In all major Canadian cities, it is controlled at the local level by elected special-purpose bodies generally known as school boards. Friction between school boards and municipalities seems endemic.[15] The form it takes depends on such matters as the education-financing regimes of the various provinces and on whether there is pressure to close schools in older areas or build them in newer ones. Debates about local-government restructuring often ignore school boards, either because they are seen as untouchable or because it is assumed their boundaries can be made to adjust to new municipal structures after the fact.

We are constantly reminded that schools in general are crucial for Canada's future economic growth. But what is sometimes forgotten in Canada – although rarely in the US – is that the quality of a local public school system can be crucial in attracting new residential growth and, in some circumstances, even new businesses. People concerned with truly integrated approaches to local economic growth must never forget the potential importance of the local governments that control our schools. In recent years, the notion that local networks of schools still should be governed by their own elected special-purpose authorities, the origins of which date back to before Confederation, is increasingly under attack. Significant diminutions in school-board policy-making and taxing authority have already occurred in Quebec, New Brunswick, Nova Scotia and Alberta. Ontario's Fair Tax Commission has made similar proposals. In none of these cases, however, has much thought been given to more closely integrating the governance of schools with that of the municipalities in which they are located.

Except for education, most of the remaining functions listed in table 1 relate to property: servicing it, protecting it and enabling people to get from place to place. Most of these functions in one way or another are under the jurisdiction of municipal governments, as opposed to other elected bodies, but there is still considerable debate about whether municipal councils should have direct control in such areas as policing and libraries or whether there should be some intermediary body protecting the more politically sensitive local services from the untrammelled interference of meddling local councillors.

It has often been noted that Canadians tend simply to assume that municipal government must be about property. Perhaps they do so because almost all the locally generated revenue used to pay for local-government services derives from the municipal tax on real property.[16] In any event, the view that municipal government is the government for property is not the usual one in other advanced industrialized democracies, especially not in Europe. There, municipalities are more often seen as the mechanism through which the services of the centrally controlled welfare state are actually delivered. In Canada, perhaps because provinces rather than municipalities have been the main agencies of the welfare state, social class has never been a major factor in municipal politics. Efforts by business elites to use municipalities as facilitators of economic growth have therefore never been dogged by ideological debates about whether or not municipalities should be more concerned with redistributing resources to the poor and disadvantaged. In recent years, new issues that transcend class interests – such as environmentalism and feminism – have increasingly been added to the municipal agenda.[17] Their ultimate effect on local economic development has yet to be determined.

In environmental disputes, municipalities constantly must decide between roads and neighbourhoods, between new subdivisions and nature preserves. But it is not at all clear that the imperatives of economic growth and development *necessarily* call for new construction whenever the alternative is the preservation of whatever already exists. A decision, for example, to save old buildings from destruction by an unimaginative developer could be a crucial factor in the economic renewal of a traditional downtown shopping area. If we believe that individual municipalities are capable of developing genuinely unique strategies for their own local economic development, it is decisions on exactly these sorts of issues that are likely to demonstrate what the strategy really is. If we want to know how local politicians really see their municipality's economic future, we should pay far more attention to analyzing these decisions than to reading abstract declarations of principle contained in strategic plans and vision statements.

Municipal governments are only a part of the larger system through which the Canadian state acts to affect all aspects of life in our cities.[18] In many respects their role in the current system is not as great as some elected local politicians and their senior administrators and consultants might occasionally proclaim. But because municipalities do have such a major role in determining how we use and tax our land, they are inevitably significant actors in any attempt to reinvigorate the economic life of our city-regions. With more functional jurisdiction and greater success in coordinating policy initiatives across different municipal departments, their potential role in local economic development could be much greater. Some would argue, however, that the potential can never be fulfilled unless current municipal structures and boundaries are significantly reorganized to match the territorial reality of our city-regions.

The Structural Variables

There are three different kinds of Canadian municipalities: "single-tier," "upper-tier" and "lower-tier." Within the boundaries of a single-tier municipality, there is no other municipal government. In short, a single-tier municipality is responsible for all local-government functions within its territory that are not assigned to designated local special-purpose bodies. All municipalities outside Ontario, Quebec and British Columbia (and some inside Ontario) are, by this definition, single-tier.

The other two kinds of municipalities exist within two-tier systems of municipal government. In such systems, there is one municipal government – the upper tier – responsible for a range of municipal functions thought to require a larger territory than other municipal functions. The range might include, for example, regional planning, water supply and sewage, policing and garbage disposal. In Ontario and Quebec, upper-tier municipalities go by such names as counties, regions and urban communities. British Columbia's regional districts serve roughly the same purposes as upper-tier municipalities in Ontario and Quebec, although many in BC would be reluctant to consider them as full-fledged municipalities. (Reasons for this reluctance will be briefly explored in chapter 4.)

Wherever there is an upper-tier municipality, there is, by definition, a group of lower-tier municipalities sharing the same territory. Lower-tier municipalities are usually concerned with the more local of municipal functions: zoning, recreation, garbage collection. They generally share the same designations as many single-tier municipalities throughout the country: city, town, township, parish, village.

Upper-tier municipalities differ from special-purpose bodies because they are multi-purpose. They are assigned a relatively wide range of governmental functions. Their governing councils can be made up in a number of different ways. Effective in late 1994, Ottawa-Carleton's council will comprise members elected solely to serve at the upper tier. In most upper-tier municipalities in Ontario and Quebec, the councils comprise members directly elected to serve at both tiers. In Metropolitan Toronto and Niagara, some members serve only at the upper tier and others (mayors of lower-tier municipalities) are directly elected to serve at both levels. Because BC's regional districts contain some areas that are otherwise not incorporated into municipalities, the membership of their councils (or boards of directors) is made up of some members elected directly from the unincorporated areas and of others who are the delegates of the constituent municipalities. In Quebec, Ontario and BC, there are in some cases provisions for weighted votes to reflect the widely varying numbers of people represented by different members. Debates about the nature of the system for political representation often become so heated and protracted that they prevent serious analysis of what these upper-tier municipalities actually accomplish.

The three types of *municipality* – single-tier, upper-tier, and lower-tier – exist within two types of *municipal systems:* one-tier and two-tier. For the rest of this study we shall be more concerned with distinguishing between the two types of municipal systems rather than the three types of municipalities. Indeed, whether a system is one-tier or two-tier is one of the two main structural variables to be used throughout the rest of this study.

The other variable is whether the system is "comprehensive" or not. What is being examined here is the extent to which the central single-tier or the central upper-tier municipality encompasses the overall population of the relevant city-region. Unlike the clear difference between one- and two-tier municipal systems, there are obviously degrees of comprehensiveness. Nevertheless, for the purposes of this study, Canada's 23 city-regions will be classified as being governed by a municipal system that is either territorially "comprehensive" or "non-comprehensive."

For a one-tier system to be considered comprehensive, it must include at least 70 percent of the population of the entire city-region. For a two-tier system to be so classified, the required percentage is 90. As we shall see later, given the various levels of comprehensiveness within the two types of systems, these numbers represent natural dividing points. It makes sense that the requirement for a two-tier system would be higher: one of the main reasons for having such a system in the first place is so there is one level of municipal government that at least has some capability to plan and service the city-region as a whole.

Using these two sets of twin variables creates the simple matrix shown in table 2. In the four chapters that follow, the contents of each of the four cells will be explored in some detail. In most cases, two different city-regions in each category will be examined as case studies.

Criteria for Assessment

Since the main object of this project is to assess the various structural arrangements in terms of their compatibility with local economic development, it is

table 2
distribution of types of municipal systems
among canada's 23 city-regions

	Territorial coverage		
	Comprehensive	Non-comprehensive	Totals
One-tier	8	3	11
Two-tier	8	4	12
Totals	16	7	23

important to set out the general criteria by which the assessment will be carried out. A detailed list of criteria is unfortunately impossible. This is because there is unlikely to be agreement about which criteria are important for economic development and which are not. Some observers will stress the importance of low levels of taxation; others the importance of certain kinds of services. Some will correctly point out that the relative importance of government policies as a whole will vary according to what type of economic-development strategy is pursued. Measuring the extent to which different systems meet the various criteria would also be exceptionally difficult.

Notwithstanding the difficulties of assessment outlined above, we can suggest that, in order for municipal structures to be compatible with economic development, they must promote both *efficiency* and *effectiveness*. Each of the structural arrangements outlined in this paper will therefore be assessed in these terms.

Efficiency has to do with limiting waste, with making maximum use of available resources. By definition, waste leads to unnecessarily high levels of taxation and/or low levels of service, both of which, other things being equal, affect economic development, directly and indirectly. The causes of waste in government are in dispute. Some argue that waste results primarily from governments (or their agencies) that are too small for the task at hand. The result is the existence of too many governments all trying to do the same thing, often in wasteful competition with each other. Citizens do not know who is responsible for what and can hold no one politically accountable. The solution is to consolidate many governments into one, thereby eliminating duplication and providing a single accountable authority.

For others, however, it is precisely the large size and monopoly position of government that causes inefficiency. Just as monopolies in the private sector grow fat, inefficient and exploitative, so do large governments. For proponents of this viewpoint, the notion that voters can ensure efficiency through the ballot box is a fiction. Voters can never have enough information to curtail the inevitably self-serving actions of incumbent politicians and bureaucrats. In this view, governments are best made accountable – and therefore efficient – by forcing them to compete with other governments to attract taxpayers and investment. Far from being inefficient, a network of small overlapping, competitive governments is – according to this "public-choice" view – the best mechanism for promoting overall governmental efficiency. Creating and fostering such networks is, therefore, a valid public policy objective.

No attempt is made in this study to determine which of these conflicting views is closest to the truth in any given set of circumstances. Instead, each particular set of structural arrangements will be assessed according to the extent to which it has the potential to promote efficiency either through *political accountability* or through the *discipline of the marketplace.*

Effectiveness has to do with achieving objectives. The more an organization is successful in reaching its objectives, the more effective it is said to be. Organizations can be effective without being efficient, or efficient without being effective. With the exception of those who wish to keep the role of government to an absolute minimum, most Canadians, other things being equal, are likely to approve of the idea that government should be organized for each city-region in such a way that it at least has the *potential* to foster economic development, control and co-ordinate outward physical expansion, provide certain region-wide services and redistribute tax resources from wealthier areas to poorer areas. Without such potential, governments cannot, by definition, be successful in meeting policy objectives for the city-region as a whole. Various structural arrangements will therefore be assessed in this study according to the extent to which they have the potential to set and achieve such objectives.

Notes

1. Warren Magnusson, "The Local State in Canada: Theoretical Perspectives," *Canadian Public Administration*, Vol. 28, no. 4 (Winter 1985), pp. 575-99. For an alternative definitional approach to special-purpose bodies which excludes school boards on the grounds that they generally have the right to levy their own taxes, see David Siegel, "The ABCs of Canadian Local Government: An Overview," in Dale Richmond and David Siegel (eds.), *Agencies, Boards and Commissions in Canadian Local Government* (Toronto: Institute of Public Administration of Canada, 1994), pp. 7-9.

2. Harold Wolman and Michael Goldsmith, *Urban Politics and Policy: A Comparative Approach* (Oxford: Blackwell, 1992).

3. The OMB is a quasi-judicial body with extensive authority derived from a wide range of provincial statutes to adjudicate appeals from individuals and corporations concerning various municipal by-laws (especially relating to land-use planning), to arbitrate inter-municipal disputes and to approve municipal and school-board capital borrowing. Most other provinces have equivalent bodies, but none are as powerful as the OMB. For details, see Ian MacF. Rogers, *The Law of Canadian Municipal Corporations*, 2nd ed. (Toronto: Carswell, 1971 [updated to 1993]), chap. 34.

4. Data from Statistics Canada reproduced in Richard M. Bird and N. Enid Slack, *Urban Public Finance in Canada*, 2nd ed. (Toronto: John Wiley and Sons, 1993), p. 65.

5. Paul E. Peterson, *City Limits* (Chicago: University of Chicago Press, 1981).

6. Paul Kantor with Stephen David, *The Dependent City: The Changing Political Economy of Urban America* (Boston: Scott, Foresman, 1988), chap. 18.

7. For an analysis comparing Ontario to other jurisdictions, see Canadian Urban Institute, *Disentangling Local Government Responsibilities: International Comparisons*, Urban Focus Series 93-1 (Toronto: Canadian Urban Institute, 1993).

8. David Siegel, "Reinventing Local Government: The Promise and the Problems," in F. Leslie Seidle (ed.), *Rethinking Government: Reform or Reinvention?* (Montreal: Institute for Research on Public Policy, 1993), p. 180.

9. Andrew Sancton, "Municipal Government and Social Services: A Case Study of London, Ontario," *Local Government Case Studies*, no. 2 (London, ON: University of Western Ontario Department of Political Science, 1986), pp. 48-55.

10. For a discussion of the municipal role in the subdivision-approval process, see Ontario, Commission on Planning and Development Reform in Ontario, *New Planning for Ontario: Final Report* (Toronto: Queen's Printer, 1993), pp. 87-90.

11. See Pierre Le François, Secrétaire général de la Ville de Montréal, "Les principaux défis de la Ville de Montréal," texte d'une allocution au déjeuner-causerie ENAP-IAPC, Aylmer, Québec, le 18 mars 1993 and Jacques Léveillée, "Comments on David Siegel's Paper," in Seidle (ed.), *Rethinking Government*, p. 206.

12. This point is argued in more detail in Andrew Sancton, "Canada as a Highly Urbanized Nation: New Implications for Government," *Canadian Public Administration*, Vol. 35, no. 3 (Autumn 1992), pp. 292-96.

13. For the elaboration of this argument, see Sancton, "Canada as a Highly Urbanized Nation," pp. 281-98.

14. For details of the institutional arrangements in metropolitan Montreal, see Andrew Sancton, *Governing the Island of Montreal: Language Differences and Metropolitan Politics* (Berkeley: University of California Press, 1985), chap. 9.

15. Wade Locke and Almos Tassonyi, "Shared Tax Bases and Local Public Sector Expenditure Decisions," *Canadian Tax Journal*, Vol. 41, no. 5 (December 1993), pp. 941-57.

16. Harry M. Kitchen, *Property Taxation in Canada*, Canadian Tax Paper no. 92 (Toronto: Canadian Tax Foundation, 1992).

17. Warren Magnusson, "The Constitution of Movements *vs.* the Constitution of the State: Rediscovering the Local as a Site for Global Politics," and Caroline Andrew, "The Feminist City," both in Henri Lustiger-Thaler (ed.), *Political Arrangements: Power and the City* (Montreal: Black Rose, 1992), pp. 69-93 and 109-22.

18. Magnusson, "The Local State in Canada."

2

One Municipal Government
For One City-Region

The simplest form of municipal government for a city-region is to have one single-tier municipality covering the entire urbanized area, and perhaps the immediate hinterland as well: one city, one government. For many municipal structural reformers, this is the ultimate objective. A single municipality – according to conventional consolidationist arguments – saves costs through economies of scale, improves regional-planning capabilities and promotes equity in tax burdens and municipal services among metropolitan residents. Claims have also been made that consolidation can significantly improve the prospects for economic development.

There are two main processes in which comprehensive one-tier municipal government can be achieved: 1) through a series of incremental annexations by which the city's municipal boundaries are extended at roughly the same pace as outward urbanization; or 2) through a massive structural amalgamation of existing municipalities to create one new one. Both these processes will be explored in this chapter.

Comprehensive One-Tier Systems

In 1991, eight city-regions in Canada contained a single-tier municipality whose population comprised more than 70 percent of the overall CMA population. They are listed in table 3. The cut-off point of 70 percent was chosen because it is relatively high (in relation to the American experience at least) and because it represents a natural dividing point. The last city on the list in table 3 is Windsor, where the City of Windsor makes up 73 percent of the total population in the census metropolitan area. If the list were to be continued, the next city would be Saint John, where the corresponding percentage is only 60.

table 3

canadian census metropolitan areas (CMAs)
whose central municipalities account for more than 70 percent
of the total population, 1991

CMA	Percent of CMA population in central municipality	Total CMA population
Winnipeg	94.5%	652,354
Calgary	94.3%	754,033
Thunder Bay	91.6%	124,427
Saskatoon	88.6%	210,023
Regina	85.3%	191,692
London	79.5%	381,522
Edmonton	73.4%	839,924
Windsor	73.0%	262,075

Source: Statistics Canada, *A National Overview* (Ottawa: Supply and Services Canada), Catalogue no. 93-301

The current boundaries of Winnipeg and Thunder Bay were brought about as the result of a significant provincially imposed municipal amalgamation. The other cases all result from a series of annexations, although the experience in different cities concerning the frequency and size of these annexations, as well as the degree of public controversy generated, varied widely. The two cases to be examined in some detail in this chapter are Winnipeg and London: the first because it is the most dramatic Canadian example of comprehensive amalgamation and the second because it is an unusual and recent example of a very large annexation inspired, it seems, almost entirely by motives connected with economic development.

Winnipeg's Unicity

Winnipeg's comprehensive one-tier system, known as "Unicity," came into effect on January 1, 1972. It replaced a two-tier system comprising a Metropolitan Corporation of Greater Winnipeg and twelve lower-tier municipalities. Although introduced by the New Democratic Party (NDP) government led by Ed Schreyer, total amalgamation had long been an objective of central-city business interests convinced that "governmental fragmentation was hurting development."[1] The NDP White Paper on Unicity echoed such concerns. After noting that "more than half the people in the entire province live in the Greater Winnipeg area" and that "the greater part of all goods and services produced in the province are generated in this area," the White Paper then claimed that the area has also "become the greatest single repository of social ills within the province."[2]

The authors of the White Paper discerned a direct link between the city's problems and its structures of government:

> The lines of authority in many instances were blurred, or else duplicated. Individual citizens and development investors alike became confused and often exasperated in any attempt to unravel the complex lines of authority. And, overlaid on the inherent confusions of a two-tier system ... was, and is, the simple fact that the problems and difficulties of the urban community transcend jurisdictions and boundary lines. Yet the effective power to deal with these problems has been, and is, sharply delineated and circumscribed...[3]

The rest of the White Paper outlines new structures aimed at promoting administrative efficiency, area-wide equity in levels of municipal services and property taxes and greater opportunities for citizen participation through what were called "community committees" and "residents' advisory groups." But apart from the occasional general assertion that, when government is fragmented, "the community's human resources are dissipated, and its economic capabilities to a considerable extent squandered,"[4] there was no attempt to demonstrate in concrete terms exactly how amalgamation was supposed to promote economic prosperity. Instead, there was a detailed outline of how the new political and administrative arrangements for Unicity would be structured.

There was also a blueprint for the creation of the Ministry of Urban Affairs: a provincial department of government exclusively concerned with administering the City of Winnipeg Act and coordinating and improving "the performance of the provincial government as a whole in its relationship with the Greater Winnipeg region."[5] In the concluding pages, the White Paper returns to the theme of how these structural reforms will promote economic growth: "It is the Government's intention, in this program, to enlarge and facilitate urban Winnipeg's role as a generator of development in the province – and, indeed, its role as an urban centre within the larger Canadian context."[6] If nothing else, the Unicity White Paper is a remarkable example of the view that structures determine outcomes; the view that, if we can set up the right structures, all else will fall into place.

After Unicity's creation, most of the attention focussed on the new structures. Was a council of 51 members too large? Should the mayor be directly elected? What were the community committees really supposed to do? Did residents' advisory groups have any real influence in shaping local neighbourhoods? But there were no attempts to assess Unicity's success in creating a new climate for economic growth. Indeed, the first full-scale official review of Unicity made no reference whatever to economic development. The original White Paper had claimed, as we have seen, that governmental fragmentation squandered economic capabilities. The review, however, paraphrased that same section of the White Paper using these words: "fragmented authority ... prevented important decisions from being made and policies from being implemented."[7] The perceived connection between fragmentation and the lack of economic development had, by 1976, been apparently forgotten, if not deliberately ignored.

Ten years later, in 1986, Unicity was once more subject to review by an official committee appointed by the provincial government. Many of the same issues were described and analyzed, but the 1986 review seemed broader in its overall scope. There was at least a cursory attempt to assess Unicity's economic impact. The main conclusion was that the Unicity structure, with its many suburban councillors and large tax base, facilitated the building of suburban infrastructure, to the detriment of inner-city investment.[8]

If this assessment is correct – and it certainly matches the conventional wisdom about Winnipeg's post-Unicity development – then it illustrates remarkably well how structural reform can have unintended consequences. The authors of the Unicity scheme assumed that, by equalizing tax levels and services throughout the urbanized Winnipeg area, the relatively well-off suburbs would automatically be forced to subsidize the revitalization of the central city. But they seemed to ignore the fact that the population of the 11 suburban municipalities was greater than that of the old city of Winnipeg[9] and that suburban areas had considerably more growth potential. Assuming representation by population – which was always part of the NDP's plan – suburban domi-nance within Unicity was inevitable.

The main Unicity consultants for the Manitoba government subsequently defended themselves on this issue by arguing that suburban growth was inevitable under any set of structures and that, if one analyzes Unicity "non-growth" capital expenditures from 1972-80, "more than 80 percent of these...went to the central area, e.g., the former City of Winnipeg."[10] Since there is no doubt that low-density suburban growth was very costly, the issues in dis-pute are the extent to which it was inevitable and who should be paying the infrastructure costs. At a minimum, it would appear that the creation of Unicity facilitated suburban growth, in part by spreading the costs throughout the metropolitan area[11] rather than by concentrating them on the new residents and/or their immediate neighbours within the relatively small suburban municipalities.

A counterweight to Unicity's promotion of suburban growth has been the Winnipeg Core Area Initiative. Started in 1981 as a joint initiative of the gov-ernments of Canada, Manitoba and Winnipeg, the Initiative spent approxi-mately $180 million – $60 million from each government – toward revitalizing the inner-city area.[12] Although it is true that Unicity has been an active partici-pant, it appears that the federal government was the driving force, especially in the early days when the Liberal Minister from Winnipeg, Lloyd Axworthy, made the Initiative a personal priority.

Although the 1986 review of Unicity pointed to a lack of coordination between Unicity and the province on strategies for local economic develop-ment,[13] there is now some evidence that the situation has improved. In August 1993, *The Globe and Mail Report on Business Magazine* designated Winnipeg as one of Canada's five "best cities for business."[14] Many of the reasons for such a designation were beyond the control of local government: location, cost of liv-ing, attributes of the workforce. Premier Gary Filmon "and his tenacious young economic development team"[15] were given credit for being effective salespeople for the city as well as for the province. The equivalent group in the city was characterized as being "highly organized,"[16] while the mayor and the chief commissioner were praised for controlling expenditures and improving the city's credit rating. Despite all this, it was acknowledged that property taxes in Winnipeg "are disproportionately high compared with those of other Canadian cities."[17]

Nowhere in the magazine article is there any claim that Winnipeg might be in an advantageous position because there is only one municipal government covering most of the city-region. There is no evidence that the absence of inter-municipal conflict has made any difference to the pattern of Winnipeg's economic development over the past 20 years. Convincing evidence would be difficult, if not impossible, to collect but, given the kinds of claims made by the original proponents of Unicity, one would think that there should at least be anecdotal reports from the occasional business executive who has found relief in post-1972 Winnipeg from the dreadful burdens of municipal fragmentation. If such reports exist, they have not been reproduced in official government documents or in the academic literature.

The 1986 review of Unicity also addressed problems relating to the wider Winnipeg metropolitan area. In view of past policies favouring amalgamation and consolidation, one surprising recommendation was that the extreme western portion of the city – the Headingley area – be allowed to secede.

> [W]e perceive the area as a predominantly rural area without the status of a rural municipality. It would appear beneficial, therefore, to permit the area to pursue its rural and agricultural future as either a separate municipality or as part of an existing rural municipality. As an important asset in the Winnipeg region, rural Headingley should be given the opportunity to govern itself within the role that apparently all parties wish it to play.[18]

In 1991, the provincial government conducted a referendum among all residents and property-owners in the area. Of 1,390 persons enumerated, 1,163 (83.6 percent) voted and, of these, 1,008 (86.7 percent) supported secession and the establishment of a new rural municipality. In 1992, legislation was approved to make this possible.[19] Unicity became slightly less comprehensive than it had been before.

But other factors were also working in this direction. In 1971, the municipalities that were to comprise Unicity accounted for 99.1 percent of Winnipeg's census metropolitan area. In 1991, the figure was still high – 94.5 percent – but it had been significantly reduced. Between 1986 and 1991, the City of Winnipeg's population increased by 3.7 percent while that of the whole CMA went up by 4.3 percent. Put more dramatically, the population of the rural municipalities surrounding Winnipeg increased by 15.6 percent while the rate for Manitoba as a whole was only 2.7 percent. The City of Winnipeg contained 94.5 percent of the population of Winnipeg's CMA but, between 1986 and 1991 it accounted for only 85.4 percent of the population growth. In comparison to other Canadian city-regions, these figures for the central municipality are still very impressive, but they do indicate that, even with the most comprehensive of structural reforms, much urban-related development takes place outside the central urban municipality.

The 1986 review recognized this by recommending the establishment of a new advisory, consultative and coordinating organization linking all municipalities within the Winnipeg commutershed. The review committee made it clear that it was not recommending "a new layer of regional government as in Ontario." Nor was it recommending "another layer of bureaucracy."[20] Despite these disclaimers, the committee clearly accepted the fact that, for some municipal purposes – such as regional planning, environmental assessments and refuse disposal – the boundaries of Unicity were too limited. The new inter-municipal organization was also seen as having a role in assembling data and coordinating research relating to "economic development, industrial location, tourism ... and other relevant matters of importance to the region."[21]

In 1989 the provincial government established what is now known as the Capital Region Committee. It is co-chaired by the minister of Urban Affairs and the minister of Rural Development and it comprises the minister of the Environment, the mayors of the city of Winnipeg and the towns of Selkirk and Stonewall as well as the reeves of twelve rural municipalities. Its three goals are:

- to provide the Capital Region municipalities and the Province with a forum for the identification and discussion of regional issues, concerns, and ideas;

- to identify approaches to resolving regional issues and concerns, and to implementing solutions; and

- to work together to enhance the attractiveness and prosperity of the Capital Region.[22]

Meeting only three times between June 1991 and February 1992, the committee has been primarily concerned with developing a local strategy for sustainable development, especially solutions to the problem of "uncultivated and unused river lots in the region."[23]

The Capital Region Committee appears to be of very limited importance. Given that the City of Winnipeg is so dominant within the region and that the provincial Ministry of Urban Affairs is effectively a kind of upper-tier government for the wider Winnipeg region, this is scarcely surprising. The existence of a distinct ministry for Winnipeg might lead some to conclude that the city's autonomy is gravely compromised. In comparison with other Canadian cities, however, Winnipeg seems relatively well off.[24] One of the main objectives of the Ministry of Urban Affairs is to help ensure that the City of Winnipeg is not subject to all the various provincial rules and regulations designed for much smaller municipalities. If municipalities within other city-regions are genuinely seeking more autonomy, they might wish to explore the Manitoba model.

London's 1993 Annexation
On January 1, 1993, the territory of the City of London, Ontario almost tripled. The annexation is significant for this study not so much because of its size but because the provincial government's justification for it was so closely linked to the issue of economic development. It is not an exaggeration to state that the Minister of Municipal Affairs considered the London annexation to be an integral part of the government's strategy for Ontario's economic recovery. Rarely has any politician explicitly connected municipal structures and economic well-being in such a dramatic fashion. This examination of the London annexation controversy aims at illuminating some of the issues at stake to determine the extent to which the claims of the minister might have been justified.

Even before the 1993 annexation, London was Ontario's most populous single-tier municipality. It avoided two-tier regional government in the 1960s and 1970s because in 1962 the city annexed most of the land from adjoining townships that had already been developed around the city's borders as well as large areas of undeveloped land. In a sense the city itself became a kind of single-tier regional government in 1962, *albeit* with less rural hinterland than was assigned elsewhere to the new regional governments established during the decade that followed. By the early 1980s, however, London claimed to be running short of industrial land, while its neighbour to the south, Westminster township, began an aggressive campaign to attract industrial growth, especially in the corridor adjoining Highways 401 (Toronto-Windsor) and 402 (London-Sarnia) just outside London's city limits.

In November 1988, London made a formal application to the Minister of Municipal Affairs to begin negotiations for boundary adjustments. It was seeking 2,792 additional hectares on its northern, western and southern borders. Much of the land to the south was along Highway 401 and it was by far the most important. A key feature of the scheme was London's stated willingness to work out a contractual arrangement with what was then the Town of Westminster to provide water-supply and sewage systems for much of the town's existing industrial area. London's proposal was clear: it would abandon its policy of refusing to supply such services outside its borders in return for obtaining new industrial land along Highway 401.

Seventeen months of negotiation led nowhere. In April 1990, the Liberal Minister of Municipal Affairs concluded that the city's proposal was "not in the best interest of the area....[T]he area affected is much more extensive than identified by the City in its proposal and the issues must be approached in a more comprehensive manner."[25] The minister's letter caused the Town of Westminster to propose a form of two-tier regional government for the area and the city to extend its annexation proposal in all directions, especially in the south where it would take in all of Westminster.

By January 1991, local agreement still had not been reached. To solve the problem, the NDP Minister of Municipal Affairs appointed a local business person as "arbitrator," who was given three months to determine new local governmental arrangements for the area. His terms of reference were clearly defined. He was told that all recommendations must reflect "provincial interests," the first of which was "[o]ptimizing economic growth opportunities and growth management capabilities within the Greater London Area." In particular, the province required

> that there be a government structure, comprised of elected people and based on the principle of representation by population, with responsibility for at least planning and servicing, to cover the area reasonably anticipated to be within the City of London's area of major influence for at least 20 years, including:
>
> - future urban areas dependent upon London-centred infrastructure;
>
> - London airport [immediately to the east of existing boundaries];

- sufficient lands adjacent to the Highway 401/402 corridor.

A crucial "Note" in the terms of reference stated that

> "Regional government" for the current County of Middlesex and City of London is not a preferred option due to the availability of other growth management options, and the City's dominance when the principle of representation by population is applied.[26]

The arbitrator's report recommended the huge annexation for London – including the absorption of the Town of Westminster – that was later implemented. Here are some of the arbitrator's comments about the potential links between the annexation and economic growth:

> The Province of Ontario has identified the London area as a centre of strong economic growth and throughout the arbitration process there was continuous evidence to support this expectation.

> A city such as London requires a substantial land area in order to plan responsibly for the future. Beginning with a clearly stated vision, this planning must ensure that economic opportunities are met in a timely and financially effective manner....

> A major annexation by the City will provide it with the capability of creating economic growth for the area.[27]

> Over the past many years, Westminster has been both aggressive and creative in its efforts to become a distinct urban community. Unfortunately, it does not have the financial strength to provide significantly to the growth potential of the Greater London Area.[28]

In a statement issued when the legislation to implement the report was first made public, the minister stated that:

> The London area is one of the most desirable places in which to live and work. It has the potential to attract new commercial and industrial

development that can give a much-needed boost to its own – and the province's – economy. The reality is, however, that London cannot accommodate new growth within its existing boundaries.[29]

Few disputed the claim that London. needed more land suitable for industrial development. The real issue was the amount of land that was required.

During the arbitration process, the city increased its estimates concerning future needs. Part of the city's justification for the increase was that

> Industries are now looking for more amenities in their developments.... Many of the site searches now look for open space and wooded areas and as a result of this trend want more land for open space and landscaping on the site. This factor alone could double the demand in the future for industrial lands.[30]

Such arguments seemed to conflict with the province's claim that one of the advantages of a large annexation was that the expanded city, subject to considerable provincial control, would be held responsible for preventing the kind of urban sprawl that has in the past caused extensive environmental damage and excessive servicing costs. In any event, the city's amended projected requirements for industrial land involved only 4,742 hectares, while the whole annexation involved 26,000.

Much of the explanation for the size of the annexation is that, once it was decided to strip Westminster of its industrial area, the remaining part was not independently viable, nor was it attractive to adjoining rural townships. Despite all the rhetoric about the city being well positioned to plan and preserve its southern rural hinterland, much of the city's new agricultural land is a cost of annexation, not a benefit.

The province's policy concerning municipal governmental arrangements in London deserves careful analysis. Given its prior promotion of regional government and county restructuring, the rejection of a two-tier solution for London and Middlesex seems surprising. In many respects, however, the provincial authorities were simply confronting demographic reality. Within London's CMA, which includes the city of St.Thomas in Elgin county to the south, the central municipality in 1991 accounted for 79.5 percent of the total population of 381,522. However the boundaries of a new upper-tier authority might have been drawn, London would have been overwhelmingly dominant. The new boundaries add only about 8,000 to the city's 1991 population of 303,165.

Far more debatable than the decision not to impose a two-tier system was the province's assumption that future economic growth in the area required a single municipal government to plan and service both the already urbanized area and the Highway 401/402 corridor. The first questions arise with respect to the corridor. Are highways going to be important for the jobs of the future? Or might it be that (for London at least) proximity to teaching hospitals and/or the university is more important? Such issues were never really addressed in the debate about London's boundaries. It was simply assumed that economic growth must be centred on manufacturing and that access to major highways is crucial.

Even if such an assumption is correct, it still does not follow that new manufacturing plants need to be within city boundaries. What they need is appropriate access to labour, customers, suppliers and water and sewers. Manufacturers do not care who supplies the water and the sewers: they just want reliable service at a reasonable cost. In London's case, it was the province that ruled out Westminster's providing water and sewers on the basis of an agreement with the city of London. No reasons were ever given for such refusal apart from claims that inter-municipal agreements of this kind violated ministry policy because they made the municipal system as a whole less accountable to the taxpayer.

Ironically, from the perspective of potential new investors in the London area, a much more modest annexation might have been preferable. If London had obtained some new industrial land near the highways in return for supplying water and sewer services to Westminster, then new investors could have chosen between one municipality and the other. There would have been different property-tax rates in the two municipalities and differing levels of municipal services – fire suppression being a good example. Some might view an industry's choosing to locate for property-tax reasons just outside London's borders as parasitical on the central city. But what if London loses new investment in part because its property taxes are high in relation to an industrial suburb of Toledo, Ohio? It might be the case that investment so apparently dependent on low property taxes is not worth attracting in the first place. Or it might be that any company claiming to make locational decisions primarily on the basis of the level of property tax is only bluffing and that its main objective is to squeeze out financial concessions from whatever government has the authority to deliver them. The point is, however, that in London such issues were never addressed.

Another irony of the annexation outcome is that one of the London area's largest manufacturers – the Ford assembly plant at Talbotville – now sits just outside the city's southern boundaries. If another manufacturer wanted to locate in the same area but within the new city limits, the city could not possibly supply the required services. The area is miles from any conceivable expansion of city services in the foreseeable future. Services would have to be arranged with the province, presumably using the same systems established for Ford when its plant opened a couple of decades ago.

If there is no significant manufacturing growth in the Highway 401/402 corridor in future years, we shall know that the annexation was not necessary and that it was possibly counter-productive. If there is, we shall never know whether it would have taken place in the absence of annexation. We do know, however, that manufacturing facilities need adequate municipal services. In London, the province insisted that such services could not be provided through inter-municipal agreements and that structural change was necessary. In many other parts of Canada and in most of the US, such a position would seem incomprehensible. Why should municipal boundaries be determined by a network of underground pipes?

Assessment

The *efficiency* of one-tier comprehensive municipal systems in Canada has tended to be assumed rather than investigated. Such assumptions are partly based on the fact that consolidation, by definition, eliminates inter-municipal disputes and duplication. Unfortunately, we do not know whether or not the disputes and duplication are simply reproduced in a different form within the complex organizational apparatus of the larger municipality. In theory, we should be able to compare the costs of providing the same levels of the same services within two or more city-regions of the same size, at least one of which has only one municipality.[31] Because municipalities in most provinces rely heavily on provincial grants, and because the system of grants varies from province to province,[32] it would be almost essential that the city-regions chosen for comparative analysis be within the same province. With these constraints in place, the research enterprise becomes virtually impossible. A possible pairing within Ontario would be Hamilton and London. Such a comparison would doubtless indicate that, other things being equal, London's comprehensive one-tier system was more efficient. But most people would agree that, for Hamilton and London, other things are simply not equal. Different local economies mean different kinds of work forces, different expectations from local governments and different attitudes toward trade unions.

A much more crude measure of efficiency might be relative tax rates on property. Here the evidence for Ontario is interesting. Of the 11 largest municipalities in Ontario, London (8th largest) and Windsor (10th), have the lowest and second-lowest levels respectively of combined residential taxes and services charges.[33] Of the 11, London and Windsor are the only ones with single-tier comprehensive systems of municipal government.

London's apparent efficiency is also confirmed by two other studies. A report prepared for the Niagara Region Review Commission in 1988 examined municipal expenditures per household in London, Windsor and Thunder Bay – all comprehensive one-tier systems – and within six different Ontario regional municipalities.[34] London's per-household expenditures for 1986 were the lowest of the nine cases studied. Windsor and Thunder Bay, however, ranked fifth- and eighth-lowest respectively, thereby suggesting that London's apparent efficiency might have little to with it being a single-tier system.

In late 1992, *The Financial Times of Canada* surveyed Canada's 13 largest cities to determine in which one "taxpayers get the most for their money."[35] Two of the cities, Mississauga and Laval, are within the larger city-regions of Toronto and Montreal respectively and are therefore not relevant for the purposes of this monograph.[36] Indices were developed to measure spending and performance levels for police, fire, waste collection and disposal and transit while spending-level indices (without corresponding performance indices) were worked out for roads and general municipal administration. Each city was assigned an ordinal ranking for spending and performance (where available) for each service, producing ten different rankings altogether. The ordinals for each city were then added together. London had the lowest total and therefore was ranked as the most efficient. Of the remaining 10 city-regions, the ranking of those with single-tier comprehensive municipal systems was as follows: Calgary second, Winnipeg third and Edmonton fifth. Thunder Bay, Saskatoon, Regina and Windsor were not included in the survey.

In its analysis of why London is so apparently efficient, Mark Stevenson of *The Financial Times* notes that "[t]he city has a single tier of government, without the confusion and duplication of a metropolitan structure laid on top, as in such cities as Metro Toronto and Montreal."[37] London's mayor, Tom Gosnell is quoted as saying: "In a single-tier system, we can't hide behind different levels of bureaucracy. It's a much more accountable city, and accountability usually leads to savings for the taxpayer."[38]

On the basis of the limited data available, there seems little doubt that single-tier comprehensive systems are relatively efficient, at least in comparison to two-tier systems. To the extent that such efficiency is a function of structural arrangements (rather than size or social conditions, for example), it presumably results from the absence of inter-municipal conflict and from clear lines of *political accountability.*[39]

The Winnipeg case, however, remains a mystery. In the *Financial Times* survey, it ranked third but, as we have seen, it was considered by *The Globe and Mail Report on Business Magazine* to have property taxes which are quite high in relation to those of other Canadian cities. There can be many explanations for this apparent contradiction. One is that, unlike other Canadian cities outside Ontario and Nova Scotia, Winnipeg still pays a portion of its residents' social-assistance costs. Others are that alternative sources of revenue (provincial grants and/or fees of various kinds, including development charges or levies) are relatively low or that services not covered by *The Financial Times* (e.g., parks and recreation, libraries) are relatively costly in Winnipeg. Such considerations point to the obvious problems involved in making definitive judgments based solely on the *Financial Times* data.

Measuring *effectiveness* – defined here as the potential to bring about desired policy outcomes for the whole city-region – is even more difficult. Nevertheless, in principle it is clear that single-tier comprehensive systems are well structured for making effective region-wide decisions. There is no uncertainty about which tier is responsible for what. There is one municipality that is overwhelmingly dominant.

Difficulties are likely to arise only in relation to the municipality's outer limits. If these limits extend too far, rural areas are needlessly enmeshed in urban concerns and people on both sides of the border are frustrated by various additional costs and inefficiencies. In Winnipeg, such concerns led to Headingley's secession. If the city limits are tightly drawn around the built-up area, there is no municipal government that can effectively plan for future outward growth – hence demands for annexation.

London's Mayor Gosnell has justified his city's annexation in these words: "This gives us the chance to do long-term planning, to keep offering affordable, accessible land. That's been our great success."[40] If comprehensive single-tier municipalities use their great planning potential to shape better city-regions, then problems with the outer boundaries are trivial. Unfortunately, however, empirical investigations aimed at isolating the effects of municipal planning on the quality of our urban life are next to impossible.[41]

Notes

1. Meyer Brownstone and T.J. Plunkett, *Metropolitan Winnipeg: Politics and Reform of Local Government* (Berkeley: University of California Press, 1983), p. 30.

2. Manitoba, *Proposals for Urban Reorganization in the Greater Winnipeg Area*, December 1970, p. 2.

3. Manitoba, *Urban Reorganization*, pp. 2-3.

4. Manitoba, *Urban Reorganization*, p. 4.

5. Manitoba, *Urban Reorganization*, p. 28.

6. Manitoba, *Urban Reorganization*, p. 31.

7. Committee of Review, City of Winnipeg Act, *Report and Recommendations* (Winnipeg: Queen's Printer for Manitoba, 1976), p. 9.

8. City of Winnipeg Act Review Committee, *Final Report 1986*, p. 5. See also, Lloyd Axworthy, "The Best Laid Plans Oft Go Astray: The Case of Winnipeg," in M.O. Dickerson, S. Drabek and J.T. Woods (eds.), *Problems of Change in Urban Government* (Waterloo, ON: Wilfrid Laurier University Press, 1980) pp. 105-23.

9. Manitoba, *Urban Reorganization*, p. 12.

10. Brownstone and Plunkett, *Metropolitan Winnipeg*, p. 171.

11. There are no "development charges" or "lot levies" in Winnipeg. For a general explanation and assessment, see Enid Slack and Richard Bird, "Financing Urban Growth Through Development Charges," *Canadian Tax Journal*, Vol. 39, no. 5 (December 1991), pp. 1288-1304.

12. Winnipeg Core Area Initiative, *Revitalizing the Heart of Winnipeg: Canada-Manitoba-Winnipeg Tripartite Agreement, 1986-1991* (pamphlet).

13. Committee of Review, *Final Report 1986*, p. 33.

14. Ann Walmsley, "City Lights," *The Globe and Mail Report on Business Magazine*, Vol. 10, no. 2 (August 1993), p. 49. The other four were Moncton, Vancouver, Edmonton and Montreal.

15. Walmsley, "City Lights," p. 52.

16. Walmsley, "City Lights," p. 53.

17. Walmsley, "City Lights," p. 53.

18. Walmsley, "City Lights," p. 74.

19. Manitoba, Urban Affairs, *Annual Report 1991-92*, p. 40.

20. Review Committee, *Final Report 1986*, p. 77.

21. Review Committee, *Final Report 1986*, p. 75.

22. Urban Affairs, *Annual Report, 1991-92*, p. 38.

23. Urban Affairs, *Annual Report, 1991-92*, p. 38.

24. For a detailed discussion of provincial-municipal relations in Winnipeg, see Review Committee, *Final Report 1986*, pp. 10-20.

25. Letter dated April 25, 1990 from John Sweeney, Minister of Municipal Affairs, to participants in the London boundary negotiations.

26. Ministry of Municipal Affairs, Greater London Area Arbitrator, *Co-opportunity: Success Through Co-operative Independence* April 1992, Appendix 1.

27. Municipal Affairs, *Co-opportunity*, p. 2.

28. Municipal Affairs, *Co-opportunity*, p. 5.

29. "Statement by the Honourable Dave Cooke, Minister of Municipal Affairs, on London/Middlesex Annexation, June 18, 1992."

30. Letter from S.R. Gallagher, Economic Development Manager, City of London, dated March 19, 1992 to the Office of the Greater London Area Arbitrator.

31. Harry Kitchen has analyzed existing research on the efficient delivery of particular local-government services but he does not attempt to compare overall efficiency among identified cities. See his "Efficient Delivery of Local Government Services," *Discussion Paper*, no. 93-15 (Kingston, ON: School of Policy Studies, Queen's University, 1993). For Enid Slack's comments on an earlier version of this paper, see Ronald W. Crowley (ed.), *Competitiveness and Delivery of Public Services* (Kingston, ON.: School of Policy Studies, Queen's University, 1993), pp. 119-25.

32. For details, see Paul A.R. Hobson, "Local Government in Canada: Creature, Chameleon, Consort," in Melville McMillan (ed.), *Provincial Public Finances: Plaudits, Problems, and Prospects*, Canadian Tax Paper no. 91, Vol. 2 (Toronto: Canadian Tax Foundation, 1991), pp. 215-40.

33. London, *1993 Tax Bill Information* (pamphlet). This information is attributed to the Ontario Ministry of Municipal Affairs.

34. Ontario, Niagara Region Review Commission, *Report and Recommendations* (Toronto: Queen's Printer, 1989), p. 72.

35. *The Financial Times of Canada*, November 7, 1992.

36. Of the 13 cities, Laval was ranked fourth and Mississauga was seventh. Arguably, some of their apparent efficiency could result from "free-riding" on services provided by more central municipalities. But their efficiency ratings were hardly so spectacular as to merit any decisive conclusions.

37. *Financial Times of Canada*, November 14, 1992.

38. *Financial Times of Canada*, November 14, 1992.

39. This position is clearly stated in Canadian Urban Institute, *Disentangling Local Government Responsibilities: International Comparisons*, Urban Focus Series, no. 93-1 (Toronto: Canadian Urban Institute, 1993), pp. 82-83. The presence of economies of scale is another possible explanation. The *Financial Times* data are too sketchy to suggest any meaningful conclusions on this issue. The economies-of-scale issue is briefly addressed in the next chapter.

40. *Financial Times of Canada*, November 14, 1992.

41. For a brief discussion of the varying impacts of different kinds of planning, see N.H. Lithwick and Barbara Lippett-Clark, "Economic Development in Ottawa-Carleton," *Ottawa-Carleton Regional Review*, Research Study no. 4 (Ottawa: Carleton University Centre for Policy and Program Assessment, 1988), pp. 42-44.

3

Governing Without Reorganizing: Destructive Fragmentation or Governmental Marketplace?

In metropolitan Chicago in 1982 there were 374 incorporated cities, towns and townships. They were linked with each other politically only by a disparate array of six weak counties and 503 special districts.[1] Chicago's system of local government doubtless has its faults. But, if one were to take seriously the Canadian conventional wisdom that each city-region needs a comprehensive single-tier or upper-tier municipal government, then one would expect that Chicago simply would not function. Yet Chicago does function: roads connect municipalities to each other; sewers lead to treatment plants; buses and subways operate; and there are lots of exciting things to do and see. Investors still invest in Chicago. New jobs are created.

The fact that major city-regions can function, in some fashion at least, without a comprehensive municipal government is often forgotten by the most avid of Canadian municipal reformers. Such people fret about irrational boundaries, fragmentation, duplication and competition. They may well be justified in doing so. There are no doubt a good many urban problems that can be at least partly solved by consolidating municipal structures. But what is frustrating about the Canadian debate on such issues is that there is rarely any acknowledgment that there is a serious argument in favour of fragmentation. This view may not be influential in Canada, but it is exceptionally so in the US. Before assuming that municipal fragmentation is a municipal disaster, we should at least be made aware of the other side of the argument. That is the objective of the first part of this chapter. Then we shall go on to look at the few Canadian examples of non-comprehensive single-tier systems, focussing especially on Halifax.

The Public-Choice Defence of Municipal Fragmentation

The main objective of analysts who have adopted the "public-choice" approach is to design systems of government and public policies in such a way that individuals have the maximum freedom to use their own resources as they see fit. Notwithstanding the claims of their opponents, advocates of public choice are not in principle opposed to using government to redistribute wealth from the rich to the poor. However, they do argue that any such redistribution should be the result of a single, explicit redistributive system in which cash and/or cash-like vouchers are issued to those with incomes below a designated level. Under this system, both rich and poor supposedly maintain maximum control over their own economic fate.

Public-choice analysts believe that politicians and bureaucrats working within government are generally self-serving.[2] The best way to prevent the ill effects of such behaviour is to subject governments as much as possible to the discipline of the marketplace. One way to do this is to insist that components of government compete with the private sector: hence the pressure for privatization and contracting out. Another way – especially relevant at the municipal level – is to force governments to compete with one another. Once one considers the notion that competition among governments, like competition among retailers, might be good, then many of the arguments about the virtues of a single comprehensive government for a city-region are turned on their head.

Just as commercial retail organizations seldom produce the products they sell, public-choice analysts argue that there is no reason why a given municipal government should be expected to produce all the public services for which it is responsible. Instead, municipal governments should be seen as "arrangers" of services.[3] Production could be the responsibility of one or more of at least five different organizations: the municipality itself (a municipal service); a private firm (a contracted-out or franchised service); another government (through an intergovernmental contract); a voluntary association; or an inter-municipal special-purpose body. When municipalities are seen primarily as service arrangers rather than as producers, then the problem of ensuring that their boundaries are optimal for the production of their mix of assigned functions becomes much less problematic. Municipal boundaries can then be used to delineate real communities, and optimal boundaries for service production can be worked out by other agencies and even by the private sector.

Empirical evidence collected by public-choice analysts suggests that capital-intensive services such as water-supply and sewage systems benefit from economies of scale, at least up to a certain level of population. Thus it makes sense for the organizations responsible for the production of such services to be relatively large. But empirical evidence also suggests that there are often few, if any, economies of scale related to labour-intensive services such as policing, especially if one removes more specialized aspects of the service (training and radio communications) from routine aspects (street patrol and the investigation of traffic accidents).[4] Such evidence makes it possible for public-choice analysts to envision city-regions comprising dozens or even hundreds of municipalities, each efficiently producing a few public services for itself and arranging with other producing organizations for others.

The existence of so many municipalities is supposed to encourage differentiation in service and tax levels, thereby giving citizen-consumers a wide range of choice. Those wanting high levels of service will find a high-tax municipality able to cater to their needs. Older people might seek out municipalities offering frequent police patrols, or even checkpoints, in residential areas, while families with children would look for good schools and recreation programs. At the other end of the spectrum, many more people, either by choice or necessity, will make do with a lower level of services, but will save on their municipal taxes. Manufacturers might even be able to find municipalities with very low taxes that provide virtually no services to their few residents. The existence of such municipalities might arguably be very effective in helping create new jobs within the city-region as a whole, hence benefitting everybody indirectly.

A system of competing municipalities, in theory at least, creates a genuine municipal marketplace, complete with specialization and product differentiation. Consumers can compare municipalities offering similar services and readily determine which one is more efficient. If they live in a poorly performing municipality, they can then either take political action to change their municipality's political and/or administrative leadership or, more likely, move away, thereby contributing (other things being equal) to a lowering of property values. A central problem with public-choice analysis is determining the extent to which citizen-consumers actually do use, and respond to, available information about municipal performance. In the real world, it seems unlikely that they act as promptly and decisively as would be necessary to affect significantly the behaviour of municipal politicians and bureaucrats.

Another problem with public-choice theory in this context has to do with the assumption that a municipality's service and taxation policies will be based on the policy preferences of its voters. In the real world, residents in wealthy municipalities will indeed have such a luxury. Such residents might even be able to "export" their taxes by charging high rates to businesses which, for whatever reason (location, availability of a specialized work force) have little choice but to locate within their boundaries. Because the businesses then build the cost of their taxes into the price of their goods, the high business taxes in the wealthy municipality are ultimately paid by people residing elsewhere. In poorer municipalities, however, residents could be so desperate for new investment that they might feel forced to dramatically lower or even eliminate taxes. To the extent that businesses respond to such concessions, they end up locating in less than optimal places for overall efficiency and they avoid paying their fair share of community costs.

These problems of tax exporting, fiscal inefficiency and tax competition can be overcome through central regulation (forbidding municipal tax concessions, for example) and fiscal equalization.[5] Some public-choice advocates would no doubt object to such policies, but they are a relatively small price to pay for the prevention of potential inequities and inefficient allocations of public resources.

An equally serious problem for public-choice is the absence of any overarching governmental body able to act on behalf of the city-region as a whole. Even if we assume that such a body is not needed for service production, it may be needed for regional planning and/or economic development. Public-choice analysts tend to believe that regional planning by a single authority is probably unnecessary, and possibly harmful. They claim that those

> who formulate idealized solutions assume that they are omniscient observers who, if they could exercise omnipotent authority over the larger metropolitan community, could correct all of the inequities and solve all the problems of the area. Such a perspective ignores the calculations of ambitious persons who aspire to public office and strive to form majority coalitions in order to dominate policies that are consistent with their own aspirations and interests...The selection of a large unit

of government with a simplified structure will simply reduce the costs of gaining dominance by those who form majority coalitions. It will not produce an idealized world.[6]

This is an important point. Establishing a political structure for effective regional planning does not mean that effective regional planning will be the result. It all depends on the balance of political forces within the region. Conceivably, if there is general agreement that regional planning is necessary, it will emerge even without a regional governmental structure.[7]

Similar arguments can be made about regional economic-development agencies. If they were to have any prospect of actually changing public policy in relation to the local economy, they would have to have considerable authority.[8] But there is no guarantee that such an agency would serve equally the interests of all parts of the region. Nor, in the absence of such an agency, is there anything to stop local municipalities and businesses from working together informally to try to bring about the desired results.

Outside university economics departments, public-choice analysis has received very little attention in Canada. Public servants in provincial and local governments who have a day-to-day concern with municipal structures generally seem unaware of its existence. They certainly do not refer to it in the avalanche of reports they author. Business interests – local chambers of commerce and boards of trade – seem just as committed to organizational orthodoxy as the bureaucrats. Numerous competing businesses are meant to bring us specialization, choice and efficiency. But numerous municipal governments apparently bring us waste, duplication and overlap. Businesses themselves can work together cooperatively in local voluntary organizations but municipalities are incapable of considering anything except their own parochial interests. Since there is an almost universal acceptance of such views in Canada, the public-choice perspective is rarely aired, let alone taken seriously.

Canadians are perhaps suspicious of the public-choice approach because of its American origins. They assume that, because of the profound problems of American cities, we have nothing to learn from the US about urban governance. The American combination of multiple municipalities with the absence of state-government regulation and equalization schemes is, indeed, a public policy disaster. But arguments against municipal consolidation in Canada do not imply less provincial involvement. The current pattern of increasing provincial involvement is assumed.[9] In these circumstances, we need not fear that Canadian city-regions will become victims of the cutthroat and destructive municipal competition that causes some elite suburban municipalities to end up as armed fortresses while the central city collapses in crime and disorder.[10]

A trace of public-choice influence is to be found in the documentation generated for the Alberta Local Authorities Board (LAB) in 1980 when it considered an application from the city of Edmonton to annex all of the urbanized area around it as well as the entire county of Strathcona. About $7 million was spent by both sides for the hearings and various experts produced 12,000 pages of recorded testimony. Although Strathcona failed to convince the three-person panel from the LAB, it built much of its case on public-choice assumptions. The county's economic consultants argued that

> the present multi-municipal system could best reflect the different desires and needs of the population and be sensitive to changes in those needs over time. Conversely, a unicity form of government would, of necessity, be unable to reflect these differing needs....[11]

After the LAB approved much of Edmonton's request, the provincial cabinet stepped in to prevent the annexation of the city of St. Albert and the suburban hamlet of Sherwood Park. Nevertheless, Edmonton gained enough new undeveloped land to keep it supplied for 30 to 40 years, assuming it was to receive about three-quarters of the region's growth.[12] It is therefore highly doubtful that any provincial politicians accepted the intellectual analysis behind Strathcona's position. It is much more likely that they were simply defending themselves politically in suburban areas that were of considerable electoral importance.

Despite its reputation for free-market conservatism, Alberta shows no signs of adopting public-choice thinking concerning the organization of municipal government. Both Calgary and Edmonton qualify as having comprehensive one-tier systems. It is in Atlantic Canadian cities where public-choice advocates would feel more at home.

Non-Comprehensive One-Tier Systems

In some CMAs, the central city's share of the total population is such that it is only one player among many. There may or may not be various inter-municipal boards and commissions for particular services and functions, but there is no overall multi-functional government for the whole area. This is the most common situation found in American metropolitan areas but it is relatively uncommon in Canada. The most dramatic Canadian case is Halifax, where only 35.7 percent of the 1991 population of the CMA (320,501) lived in the central city. The other two cases are St. John's (55.7 percent of 171,859) and Saint John (60 percent of 124,981).[13]

The Moncton area is not considered a CMA by Statistics Canada because its "urbanized core" does not have a population of more than 100,000. However, it is a significant Atlantic urban centre because the total population of the "census agglomeration" is 106,503.[14] Like the three city-regions referred to above, the central city of Moncton is far from dominant. There are 11 municipalities in the agglomeration. The City of Moncton's population comprises only 52.7 percent of the total.

Moncton deserves attention because it is often cited as Atlantic Canada's greatest success story in revitalizing an urban economy.[15] Much of Moncton's economic strategy has been based on the ability of its bilingual workforce to provide telemarketing and other communications services for large parts of eastern Canada and beyond. Ironically, it is the existence of two linguistic communities in Moncton that has helped perpetuate the existence of so many municipalities. If the whole area were consolidated, francophones would comprise only about one-third of the population of the new unit. Three municipalities with francophone majorities (Dieppe, Dorchester parish and Saint-Joseph) would be eliminated, thereby weakening the institutional base of New Brunswick's important francophone minority.[16]

Instead of consolidating, municipalities in the Moncton area have formed the Greater Moncton Economic Commission so as to pool their resources concerning economic development.[17] Regardless of what the commission may or may not have accomplished, political credit for Moncton's apparent economic revival seems to have accrued to New Brunswick's Premier, Frank McKenna. It is he who is seen as the political catalyst that has enabled New Brunswick to respond quickly and effectively to changing economic circumstances. In a province with an activist urban-oriented provincial government and a population of only 724,000, the exact structural arrangements of municipal government are probably of only limited importance.

Nevertheless, over the past few years each of the governments of New Brunswick, Nova Scotia and Newfoundland has launched efforts to reorganize its local-government systems.[18] By examining in some detail the case of Halifax, an attempt is made here to determine the justifications for such reorganizations, especially as they relate to economic development.

Halifax: One Harbour, One City?

Halifax (1991 population of 114,455) was incorporated as a city in 1841. Across the harbour, Dartmouth (67,798) became an incorporated town in 1873. In 1879, the rest of the territory around the harbour and Bedford Basin was incorporated municipally as Halifax County (136,975). For the next hundred years there was considerable competition among the three municipalities to attract the industrial and commercial growth caused by Halifax's position as a crucial port and metropolis of Atlantic Canada. Calls for structural change to create some form of effective metropolitan government were frequent, especially after the Second World War.

The most comprehensive reorganization proposal was made in 1974 by the Royal Commission on Education, Public Services and Provincial-Municipal Relations, chaired by Professor John Graham, an economist at Dalhousie University. The Royal Commission cited a wide range of factors leading it to view "... Halifax, Dartmouth and their urbanizing areas as one metropolitan city ... joined, rather than divided, by its harbour.[19]

The commission then described a number of metropolitan problems, the solutions to which were apparently being blocked by the absence of a single metropolitan government. On the economic front, the commission argued that ... "municipal governments and their industrial development agencies frequently compete for new industry to the disadvantage of the province, neighbouring municipalities, and themselves."[20] It pointed out that Dartmouth, because of low taxes and ample land, often emerged the winner. Consequently, Dartmouth was reluctant to accept any of the various proposals to create a joint industrial commission for the whole area. It even attempted to block Halifax's efforts to obtain a water supply for an area that Halifax wanted to develop as a competing industrial park.[21]

The commission concluded its discussion of metropolitan economic problems in Halifax by stating that:

> Economic activity, whether port, industrial or tourism, is not being planned, promoted and developed as effectively as it would be if the

map 1
halifax-dartmouth region

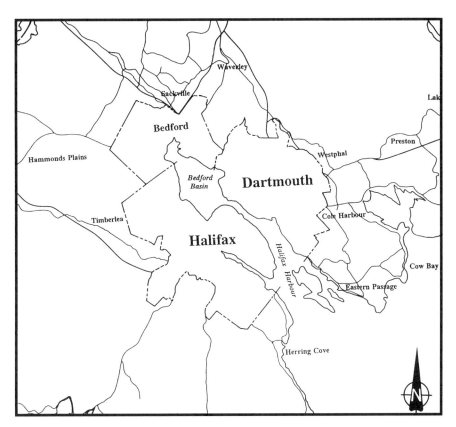

Source: Nova Scotia Department of Municipal Affairs, 1994.

area's local government powers were unified. In view of the difficulty of securing a good economic base for the area, its people cannot afford impediments put in the way by misplaced pride and resulting competition. The circumstances require cooperation, concerted effort and regional unity.[22]

After briefly examining the advantages and disadvantages of the status quo, a two-tier system and two single-tier systems, the commission recommended a single-tier system for an area roughly corresponding to that of the CMA. Ten other single-tier authorities were recommended to cover the rest of the province. So drastic were the commission's recommendations concerning municipal structures that no action was taken on any of them.

Instead, in 1980, the town of Bedford (1991 population of 11,618) was carved out of Halifax county and incorporated as a separate municipality, introducing a fourth municipal participant into the metropolitan political process. By the early 1980s it looked as though one of the area's numerous special-purpose bodies, the Metropolitan Authority, was emerging as an embryonic upper-tier metropolitan government. It was operating a regional transit system, a land-fill site and a jail.[23]

By the early 1990s, however, the province had once again become interested in major structural change. In late 1991, the Minister of Municipal Affairs created a Task Force on Local Government chaired by his deputy minister and comprising five other ministry officials, three senior municipal administrators, a financial consultant and the executive director of the Union of Nova Scotia Municipalities. It was charged with developing

> a strategy that [would] lead to the design and implementation of an appropriate form of local government for Nova Scotia in accord with existing settlement patterns that balances the concepts of economic and service-delivery efficiency with those of accountability and accessibility.[24]

In April 1992, the task force recommended that all municipal governments in the province be consolidated into the existing 18 unitary county governments, with minor boundary adjustments to be made, if necessary, during implementation. In the 46-page report, Halifax county receives only 10 lines of analysis, the conclusions being that people in the four existing municipalities "all have substantial urban populations demanding similar levels of service," that "the two cities and Bedford form a continuous band around the harbour" and that "there are very large areas of urban overspill, some of which are demanding urban-type government."[25] In late 1992, Premier Donald Cameron announced that one municipality would be created in the Halifax area in time for municipal elections scheduled for 1994. However, when Cameron was replaced as premier following the 1993 provincial election by John Savage, the former mayor of Dartmouth, the initiative appeared doomed.

Premier Cameron's policy seemed to be driven by a desire to be seen to be cutting down the size of government. Public-choice analysts would, of course, be horrified by this obvious confusion between the size of government and the number of governments, their position being that more governments at the local level are likely to lead to a reduction in the overall size of government. Such considerations have simply not been debated.

Outside government, the main advocate for consolidation in the metropolitan area is the Halifax Board of Trade, representing business interests within the city. Responding to Premier Cameron's decision to go ahead with restructuring in Halifax, the board's President stated that

> the union of the four metro municipalities is overdue and should go a long way to eliminating counter-productive inter-municipal competition.... The proliferation of unnecessary industrial parks in the four local municipalities has driven down the price of industrial land and probably presented a confusing picture to outside industries considering the region as a potential location against other North American centres.[26]

The usual claim from boards of trade and chambers of commerce about availability of industrial land is that governments have made it artificially scarce. Here we are being told that there is too much and that it is too cheap. The implication is that the existence of only one municipal government in the area would restrict the supply and cause prices to rise – exactly what public-choice analysts would argue. But the Halifax Board of Trade seems to want such a restriction, presumably because it is more concerned with the real-estate investments of its members than with encouraging the ample supply of industrial land, a state of affairs that would likely be viewed positively by potential outside investors. The board's position reminds us that, when it comes to municipal restructuring, we can never assume that proponents share the same – or even similar – political agendas.[27]

The claim by the Board of Trade that the existence of four separate municipalities creates "a confusing picture" to outside investors considering other North American locations is too absurd to be taken seriously. By North American standards, four municipalities within a metropolitan area is exceptionally low. If potential investors cannot think their way through the municipal complexities of metropolitan Halifax, they are unlikely to meet with much success in global economic competition. In any event, the four municipalities have recently managed to create a Greater Halifax Marketing Alliance, which at least provides a common brochure and telephone number for anyone making inquiries about the metropolitan area as a whole. Finally, provincial economic-development officials would always be available to investors unable to figure out the system by themselves.

Assessment

Arguments for municipal consolidation within metropolitan areas are not new. They were behind the consolidation of five counties (including the city of Brooklyn) into New York City in 1898. It is the public-choice case against consolidation that is more recent. The fact that it is more recent does not make it right, but it does mean that those arguing for consolidation should not be viewed as being on the cutting edge of municipal innovation. There is no argument for consolidation that has not been made hundreds of times before in metropolitan areas all over North America.

Even public-choice arguments are now more than 30 years old. Their appeal in the US has been one factor – although certainly not the only one – explaining why American proposals for municipal consolidation have generally not been accepted. So influential has the public-choice case become that, in 1987, one of the main organizations traditionally in support of consolidation efforts, the Advisory Commission on Intergovernmental Relations (ACIR), actually changed its position and came out in support of continued fragmentation.[28] By now public-choice analysis should be part of the intellectual equipment of any Canadian academic or provincial public servant charged with examining municipal structures. As the Halifax example shows, such is not the case. Instead, we read the same tired assertions, unsupported by empirical evidence. What is especially disturbing is that consolidation is presented as the answer not just when governments are concerned with controlling the outward expansion of the city but also when the object is to cut overall government spending.

There is no evidence that single-tier non-comprehensive systems in Canada are inefficient. In the *Financial Times of Canada* survey discussed in the previous chapter, no cities within such systems were examined. The case included in the survey that most closely approximates the single-tier non-comprehensive model is that of Vancouver, in which a weak upper-tier government includes 18 different municipalities. The City of Vancouver comprises only 29.4 percent of the population of the entire CMA. In developing its indices for Vancouver, the *Financial Times* included data not just from the City of Vancouver, but also from Burnaby, Surrey, Richmond and West Vancouver. Of the 11 cities studied in the whole survey, Vancouver was ranked sixth, ahead of Hamilton-Wentworth, Quebec City, Ottawa-Carleton, Montreal and Metro Toronto, all of which have functionally stronger upper-tier governments. Among cities with strong upper-tier governments, only the much smaller Kitchener-Waterloo-Cambridge was ranked better (fourth).[29]

The fact remains, however, that four (London, Calgary, Winnipeg and Edmonton) of the top five cities in the survey have comprehensive single-tier systems. This suggests, at a minimum, that public-choice arguments that monopoly municipal providers are inherently inefficient simply are not proven in the Canadian context. If anything, it would appear, on the basis of this flimsy evidence, that municipal *efficiency* in Canada is indeed promoted through clear *political accountability* rather than through *the discipline of the marketplace.* But efficiency deriving from direct political accountability should never be assumed. The greatest contribution of public-choice analysis is to force us to prove such claims, rather than treat them as axiomatic.

Advocates of public choice have no interest in creating a unit of local government with the potential to take effective action on behalf of the entire city-region. They are simply not interested in *effectiveness* as it is defined for this monograph. But effective government action for an entire city-region does not necessarily derive from a multi-functional municipal government. The case of Moncton illustrates the potential role of both the provincial government and of inter-municipal special-purpose bodies dedicated to a particular function.[30] In difficult economic times – when the costs of creating elaborate new institutions are likely to be prohibitive – there is much to be said for relying either on what we already have (the provincial government) or on simple structural modifications (special-purpose bodies). The mere creation of new local-governmental structures for entire city-regions does not in itself lead to predictable and desired changes in political decision making. Students of Canadian metropolitan and regional governments should by now be fully convinced of such an elementary proposition.

Public-choice analysis can help us understand much of what happens when good political intentions concerning local-government structural reform produce undesirable and unintended consequences. In making such an acknowledgment we need accept neither the ideological underpinnings of public choice nor many of its dubious implications for public policy. By introducing public-choice discourse into the debate about how our city-regions are to be governed, we are simply taking full account of all the relevant factors

Notes

1. George C. Hemmens and Janet McBride, "Planning and Development Decision Making in the Chicago Region," in Donald N. Rothblatt and Andrew Sancton (eds.), *Metropolitan Governance: American/Canadian Intergovernmental Perspectives* (Berkeley, CA: Institute of Governmental Studies Press, 1993), p. 117.

2. The most influential proponent of this view has been William A. Niskanen. For a comprehensive appraisal, see André Blais and Stéphane Dion (eds.), *The Budget-Maximizing Bureaucrat: Appraisals and Evidence* (Pittsburgh: University of Pittsburgh Press, 1991).

3. This is the same argument made by David Osborne and Ted Gaebler when they urge that governments "steer" rather than "row." The case is made in their influential bestseller, *Reinventing Government* (New York: Penguin, 1993), chap. 1.

4. For a summary of the relevant research and for a clear statement of the case for small, competitive local governments, see Vincent Ostrom, Robert Bish and Elinor Ostrom, *Local Government in the United States* (San Francisco: ICS Press, 1988), pp. 97-99 and chap. 7. See also L.J. Sharpe, "The Failure of Local Government Modernization in Britain: A Critique of Functionalism," in Lionel Feldman (ed.), *The Politics and Government of Urban Canada*, 4th ed. (Toronto: Methuen, 1981), pp. 327-30 and Christopher Hood, *Administrative Analysis* (Brighton, England: Wheatsheaf, 1986), pp. 94-100.

5. Paul A.R. Hobson, "Efficiency and the Local Public Sector," *Discussion Paper*, no. 93-21 (Kingston, ON: Queen's University School of Policy Studies, 1993). For Robert Young's comments on an earlier version of this paper, see Bryne Purchase (ed.), *Competitiveness and Size of Government* (Kingston ON: Queen's University School of Policy Studies, 1993), pp. 81-85.

6. Ostrom, Bish and Ostrom, *Local Government*, pp. 70-71.

7. Victor Jones and Donald N. Rothblatt, "Governance of the San Francisco Bay Area," in Rothblatt and Sancton (eds.), *Metropolitan Governance*, pp. 375-431.

8. For a proposal to create powerful Metropolitan Development Corporations backed by a National Metropolitan Economic Development Banking System, see N. Harvey Lithwick and Rebecca Coulthard, "Devolution and Development: The Urban Nexus," in Susan D. Phillips (ed.), *How Ottawa Spends, 1993-94* (Ottawa: Carleton University Press, 1993), pp. 257-89.

9. For the view that provincial resolve to promote inter-municipal equity within Canadian cities might be weakening, see Frances Frisken, "Canadian Cities and the American Example: A Prologue to Urban Political Analysis," *Canadian Public Administration*, Vol. 29, no. 3 (Autumn 1986), pp. 345-76.

10. For elaboration, see Andrew Sancton, "Policymaking for Urban Development in American and Canadian Metropolitan Regions," in Rothblatt and Sancton (eds.), *Metropolitan Governance*, pp. 1-12.

11. County of Strathcona, *Summary and Concluding Argument*, Strathcona Annexation Project (September 1980), p. 59.

12. Ted E. Thomas, "Edmonton: Planning in the Metropolitan Region," in Rothblatt and Sancton (eds.), *Metropolitan Governance*, p. 274. See also, Peter J. Smith and Patricia E. Bayne, "The Issue of Local Autonomy in Edmonton's Regional Planning Process: Metropolitan Planning in a Changing Political Climate," in Frances Frisken (ed.), *The Changing Canadian Metropolis: A Public Policy Perspective*, Vol. 2 (Berkeley, CA: Institute of Governmental Studies Press, 1994), pp. 725-50.

13. Statistics Canada, *A National Overview* (Ottawa: Supply and Services Canada, 1992), 1991 Census of Canada, catalogue number 93-301.

14. 1991 *Census of Canada.*

15. Moncton is the only city to be named both in 1992 and 1993 by *The Globe and Mail Report on Business Magazine* as one of Canada's top five cities in which to do business. See August 1993 issue, p. 51.

16. Léopold Chiasson, "A Prescriptive Analysis of the Local Government Restructuring in the Province of New Brunswick," University of Western Ontario Department of Political Science MPA Research Report, 1993.

17. For details, see J. E. Louis Malenfant and John C. Robison, *Greater Moncton Urban Community: Strength Through Cooperation*

(Fredericton: New Brunswick Ministry of Municipalities, Culture and Housing, April 1994), pp. 64-67.

18. Allan O'Brien, *Municipal Consolidation in Canada and its Alternatives* (Toronto: ICURR Press, 1993), pp. 13-26.

19. Royal Commission on Education, Public Services and Provincial-Municipal Relations, *Report*, Vol. 5 (Halifax: Queen's Printer, 1974), pp. 117-20.

20. Royal Commission on Education, p. 125.

21. Royal Commission on Education, p. 128.

22. Royal Commission on Education, p. 129.

23. David M. Cameron and Peter Aucoin, "Halifax," in Warren Magnusson and Andrew Sancton (eds.), *City Politics in Canada* (Toronto: University of Toronto Press, 1983), p. 185.

24. Nova Scotia, Ministry of Municipal Affairs, Task Force on Local Government, *Report to the Government of Nova Scotia*, (April 1992), p. 5.

25. Halifax, Task Force on Local Government, pp. 28-29.

26. Halifax Board of Trade, *The Voice*, Vol. 3, no. 1 (February 1993), p. 2.

27. For further discussion of the advantages and disadvantages of municipal competition in metropolitan Halifax for the supply of industrial land, see Hugh Millward and Shelley Dickey, "Industrial Decentralization and the Planned Industrial Park: A Case Study of Metropolitan Halifax," in Frisken (ed.), *The Changing Canadian Metropolis*, Vol. 2, pp. 768-71.

28. Michael Keating, *Comparative Urban Politics: Power and the City in the United States, Canada, Britain and France* (Brookfield, VT: Edward Elgar, 1991), p. 111.

29. Mark Stevenson, "Where Taxpayers Get the Most for Their Money," *The Financial Times of Canada*, November 7, 1992, p. 11.

30. A recent study did not recommend any major changes in municipal boundaries and functions – only the creation of a Greater Moncton Service Board to act "as the formal mechanism for coordinating those services currently provided jointly, as well as new regional initiatives...." See Malenfant and Robison, *Greater Moncton*, p. 38.

4

The Two-Tier Model

Canadians know all about two-tier government. We know that the upper-tier federal government in Ottawa is supposed to look after national concerns while the 10 provincial governments are responsible for more parochial matters. In two-tier municipal systems the basic principles are the same: the upper tier looks after concerns that are common to the whole region – water supply, sewers, major roads, regional planning – and the lower tier is concerned with such matters as zoning and neighbourhood parks and recreation. The general advantages and disadvantages of two-tier government are well known. Their great strength is their ability to centralize some government functions while at the same time decentralizing others. This provides a degree of integration at the centre while enabling the constituent units to protect their identity and to experiment with innovative types of policy responses depending on local conditions and preferences. The main weaknesses of two-tier systems are that they produce endless discussions about which level should be doing what and generate frequent complaints about apparent duplication, overlap and lack of coordination.

The main difference between two-tier municipal systems and the Canadian two-tier federal system has to do with the treatment of territorial boundaries. In municipal systems, the boundaries of both the upper-tier authority and the constituent parts are almost always open for discussion. In the many recent debates about Canadian federalism (if not in debates about the implications of Quebec's possible secession), boundaries are usually considered inviolate.

Comprehensive Two-Tier Systems

Starting with the creation of the Municipality of Metropolitan Toronto in 1953, Canada has developed a world-wide reputation for its two-tier systems of urban government. The three largest Canadian provinces – Ontario, Quebec and British Columbia – now have restructured two-tier systems covering most if not all of the populated parts of their respective territories. But each provincial system is quite different.

Since one of the central purposes of having a two-tier system in the first place is to include an entire metropolitan area within a common set of governmental arrangements, a two-tier system will not be considered comprehensive for the purposes of this study unless it includes 90 percent of the population of its census metropolitan area. Table 4 lists, in descending order of the extent to which its upper-tier local government covers its population, the qualifying CMAs and their 1991 populations. Ninety percent is a natural dividing point because, if the list were to be continued beyond Sherbrooke, the next entry would be Quebec City, for which the equivalent percentage is only 75.9.

table 4
canadian census metropolitan areas (CMAs) whose central upper-tier municipalities account for more than 90 percent of the total population, 1991

CMA	Percent of CMA population in central municipality	Total CMA population
St. Catharines-Niagara	108.1%[1]	364,552
Chicoutimi-Jonquière	107.4%	160,928
Victoria	104.0%	287,897
Kitchener	103.6%	356,421
Sudbury	102.3%	157,613
Trois-Rivières	100.8%	136,303
Vancouver	96.3%	1,602,502
Sherbrooke	91.4%	139,194

Source: Statistics Canada, *A National Overview* (Ottawa: Supply and Services Canada), Catalogue no. 93-301.

[1] Some percentages exceed 100 because the boundaries of the relevant upper-tier municipality extend beyond the boundaries of the census metropolitan area.

The issues for these systems relate mainly to the translation of theory into practice. Does real regional planning actually take place? How are the lower-tier municipalities represented on the upper tier? To what extent is there conflict or co-operation between the two tiers, especially involving services related to economic development? Does the system serve to redistribute resources from wealthier municipalities to poorer ones?

In this chapter, case studies are taken from two quite different two-tier systems: Ontario and British Columbia. St. Catharines-Niagara is chosen because it is the location of one of the oldest and most highly developed of Ontario's regional governments and because its territorial comprehensiveness in relation to its CMA is the greatest of any Canadian municipal government. Another reason for choosing St. Catharines-Niagara as a case study is that it has been thoroughly studied by three different Ontario government commissions. Material produced by these commissions – especially the latest – enables us to explore in depth some of the complex operational issues involving two-tier municipal systems in which both tiers have substantial authority. Since so much of municipal government is concerned with detailed problems concerning implementation, any attempt to assess municipal structures must inevitably confront such details, as well as the grand issues of principle.

Vancouver is examined in this chapter because of its inherent importance as Canada's third largest city-region and because its relatively weak and flexible upper-tier of municipal government – the Greater Vancouver Regional District – deserves more attention from students of Canadian city government than it has generally received.

St. Catharines-Niagara

In 1969, the Ontario legislature enacted a law creating the Regional Municipality of Niagara. The two counties of Welland and Lincoln and 26 other municipalities were reduced to one regional municipality and 12 lower-tier municipalities. The regional council was made up of 29 members, including a chair (initially appointed by the province, then by the other regional councillors), all 12 mayors and 16 other members elected to serve only at the regional level from wards that did not cross municipal boundaries. Functions of the regional municipality included social services, capital borrowing, main arterial roads, regional planning, economic development for the region as a whole, water and sewage treatment

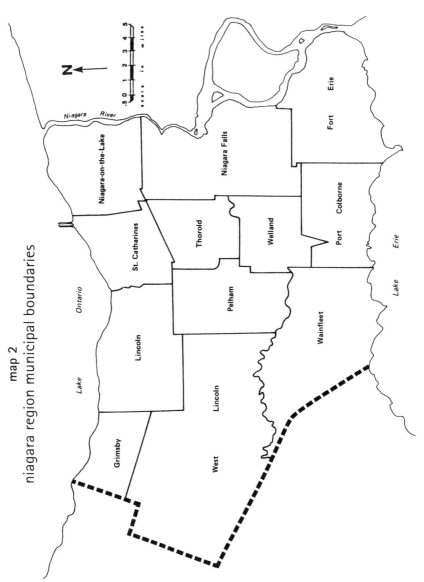

map 2
niagara region municipal boundaries

Source: Ministry of Municipal Affairs, Niagara Region Review Commission, *Report and Recommendations* (Toronto: The Queen's Printer for Ontario, 1989), p. 296.

and emergency planning. Other services, notably police, were provided by regional special-purpose bodies.

The early years of regional government in Niagara have been described as "tempestuous."[1] Discontent was especially evident within St. Catharines. The city was under-represented in terms of population within the regional council but its initial share of regional expenses was significantly more than its share of the regional population and even of regional assessment. Residents of St. Catharines also experienced higher water rates as a result of regional government, while many residents in other municipalities saw theirs decrease. Conversely, residents of the smaller, more rural municipalities began to pay for police for the first time even though most of the actual work of the new regional force remained within the urban areas.[2] Conflicts between the two tiers of government over planning and transportation issues seemed endemic. Despite high initial expectations, a common regional identity failed to emerge; regional council seemed remote from the voters and the area municipalities and incapable of playing a major role in shaping the region's future.[3]

Since its creation, the regional government system in Niagara has been subjected to two full-scale public reviews, one completed in 1977 and the other in 1989. The latter was conducted by Professor Harry Kitchen of Trent University, an expert on municipal finance who has also carried out research relating to the role of Ontario municipalities in promoting economic development.[4] The Kitchen commission addressed a wide range of issues relating to two-tier municipal systems in general and Niagara region in particular. Two of them – inter-municipal cooperation and the role of each tier in relation to economic development – are especially relevant for the subject matter of this project and will be addressed in some detail.

Inter-Municipal Co-operation. In a two-tier system, one of the reasons for creating the upper tier in the first place is to minimize the need for cooperation and agreement among the municipalities within the area covered by the upper-tier authority. Generally speaking, those functions which would otherwise require such cooperation and agreement are placed within upper-tier jurisdiction. The problem, however, is that some functions – especially land-use planning and public works – cannot be allocated entirely to one level or the other. Instead, they invariably become "shared" jurisdictions. For this arrangement to work, there must still be cooperation between each individual lower-tier municipality and the regional authority. For Niagara, the Kitchen commission explored the status of such cooperation quite thoroughly.

For land-use planning, consultants hired by the commission discovered that even among many of the politicians and staff directly involved, there was considerable confusion about who was responsible for what:

> The issue of what are regional and what are local responsibilities forms the basis for much of the dissatisfaction noted in the municipal interviews. Several people stated specifically that these responsibilities were not clearly defined. Clarification would do much to eliminate the overlap and frustration which result from the duplication of services and energy.[5]

Neither the consultant nor the commissioner was willing himself to provide such clarification. Instead the commission recommended that a joint technical planning committee, comprising staff from the region and all lower-tier municipalities, be created to resolve the confusion, subject of course to approval by the appropriate political authorities.[6]

One of the most important regional planning functions is to prepare a regional official plan. A study prepared for the Kitchen commission reported that, as of 1988, important details of the plan were still not in force because they had not yet been approved by the provincial government.[7] One of the recommendations of the commission itself was that the official plans of the region and the area municipalities be brought into conformity with each other:

> Without this conformity, the opportunity exists for problems and difficulties whenever recommendations must be made on issues having both regional and local significance. More importantly, this lack of conformity can lead to uneven standards being applied across the region and to situations where a lack of coordinated plans creates an environment in which citizens are occasionally given the "run around" in seeking approval for planning requests.[8]

What makes this commentary notable is that it was written 18 years after the establishment of the regional government, one of the main initial purposes of which was to ensure that local planning policies were in accord with an approved regional plan.

The Kitchen commission also conducted a detailed examination of inter-municipal cooperation in the field of public works. Its consultant's report noted some "tangible examples" of such cooperation: the lower-tier (area) municipalities provide maintenance services for regional (upper-tier) storm sewer mains and the region provides maintenance services for area water-supply pumping stations and local traffic signals.[9] Such cooperation is necessary because responsibility for sewers, water supply and traffic is split between the two levels. Concerning water supply and sewers, the consultant seemed satisfied that split jurisdiction did not present major difficulties.

For the commissioner, however, cooperation was not good enough. He argued that lower-tier municipalities have "relatively little incentive" to be concerned about leaks in, and improper or illegal connections with, water-supply pipes and sewage systems.[10] He suggested that the upper-tier authority "should assume complete responsibility for all aspects of the entire water, sewage and storm drainage system" so as to promote "a more efficient, environmentally acceptable, and less costly system."[11] Complete upper-tier responsibility for water supply and sewers already exists in the Durham, Halton and Peel regions and is being legislated for Ottawa-Carleton. The logic in all these cases is that inefficiencies result from split jurisdiction. The same line of reasoning leads to the wider conclusion that two-tier municipal government is itself inherently inefficient. Indeed, Professor Kitchen concludes his report by suggesting that in the long run a one-tier regional government for all of Niagara is the ideal solution.[12]

Economic Development. More so than other reports on local-government structures and functions in Canada, the Kitchen report is openly sceptical about the role of municipalities in affecting the pattern of economic development within their boundaries. In 1988, the commission contacted 27 firms that had located in the Niagara region in the recent past. Twelve responded to the questionnaire. Of these, nine reported that no government at any level had any impact on its locational decision. A similar survey of 91 firms that had recently expanded their operations in Niagara drew 28 responses. Of these, 20 claimed that "local government officials and/or politicians" played no role in their investment decision. Twenty-two claimed that the Niagara Region Development Commission (NRDC) – an agency of the regional municipality – was similarly irrelevant. Seventeen claimed that other levels of government had no influence on their decision to invest further in the area.[13] These data reinforced Kitchen's previously published view that municipal efforts to promote local economic development were unlikely to be effective.

Nevertheless, Kitchen realized that "it is probably irrational to suggest that one government terminate this activity." The political imperatives to be seen to be trying to improve the local economy are too overwhelming. Concerning the NRDC, Kitchen claimed that the strongest argument in its favour is that

> other municipalities in the province and elsewhere have similar agencies. However, considerable uncertainty over whether the NRDC is directly responsible for success in fostering and promoting economic development suggests that its budget should be monitored closely and not allowed to expand without careful scrutiny.[14]

Kitchen's doubts about the utility of much of what goes on in municipal economic development offices are shared by many other informed observers. In this sense, the limited data he generates for Niagara could probably be replicated in just about any Canadian municipality – and even in many American ones, where opportunities to offer tax concessions and other forms of inducements are much greater. An obvious question arises: why do local politicians continue to spend money to attract new investment when the objective evidence suggests that it makes no difference?

Harold Wolman has worked out a systematic answer to this question.[15] Politicians spend money to attract investment because it is a kind of political insurance policy. From a political point of view, attracting investment by spending money is the best possible outcome: the policy appears to produce results. Not spending money and obtaining investment anyway is the best outcome from an economic cost/benefit perspective, but it brings little or no political return. The opposite (spending money and not attracting investment) makes no sense economically but politicians are seen at least to be trying. Not spending money and not obtaining investment is the worst possible outcome from a political perspective, especially if the investment goes to a nearby municipality where money is being spent. As long as voters believe that spending money to attract investment is a worthwhile gamble, it makes sense for politicians seeking re-election to spend the money, even if they know that it is unlikely to produce results.

From a municipality's point of view, the decision by a major company to locate within its boundaries a manufacturing facility, research establishment or other major office complex is like winning a lottery. Some might equate spending money to attract investment with buying a ticket for the lottery. In reality, however, it is unlikely that this kind of lottery requires a ticket – but municipalities buy one just in case.

As long as municipal spending to attract investment does not amount to much, little harm is done. Professor Kitchen's recommendation – for Niagara and by implication for elsewhere – is that such spending be closely monitored. Expecting local politicians to do the monitoring is not very realistic, especially in light of Wolman's analysis, as described above. Provincial governments can regulate municipal taxation policy and most other forms of inducements to businesses, but regulating municipal advertising and other forms of promotion is likely to cause more trouble than it is worth. Ultimately, control of such spending must rest with the voters. It is their money to save.

Spending money to attract investment is not the only way in which municipalities can foster local economic development. In the long term, the most effective means of achieving such an objective is to use municipal resources and authority to create the kind of community in which people want to live and invest. In other words, a policy for local economic development involves, above all, the provision of efficient and effective municipal government. Whether two-tier systems of the kind established for Niagara are capable of being efficient and effective in some overall sense is the central question of this chapter. But before considering it, we must examine a quite different variety of two-tier municipal government.

Vancouver

Until 1965, inter-municipal services in metropolitan Vancouver were largely handled by special-purpose bodies: a Joint Sewerage and Drainage Board, a Greater Vancouver Water District, various health and hospital boards, a Lower Mainland Regional Planning Board and an Industrial Development Commission of Greater Vancouver. Between 1965 and 1967, the British Columbia government implemented a system of regional districts for the entire province, including those areas not contained within incorporated municipalities. The regional district for Vancouver, created in 1967, took over the functions of the special-purpose bodies.[16] Indeed, the provincial government was anxious to emphasize that a new level of government was not being created. It was more a matter of tidying up the existing system and creating a framework for increased municipal cooperation.

Regional districts in BC differ from regional government in Ontario in the following ways: the district's governing body is called a "board of directors" not a "council"; some members have multiple votes depending on the size of their municipalities; member municipalities can opt out of many district functions; districts provide different functions for different areas within their boundaries, especially for unincorporated areas; all municipal representatives on district boards of directors, including the chair, are elected members of municipal councils and there is no expectation that this will or should change; districts were created without changing any existing municipal boundaries – i.e., there was no simultaneous lower-tier consolidation. In short, the creation of regional districts has been much less disruptive to the traditional pattern of municipal government. Since 1984, another difference has been that regional districts no longer have any statutory authority relating to land-use planning. The authority was removed by a Social Credit provincial government anxious to promote development rather than regulate it.[17]

The Greater Vancouver Regional District (GVRD) comprises the entire Vancouver CMA except the municipalities of Pitt Meadows and Maple Ridge. Pitt Meadows (1991 population of 11,147) already participates in the GVRD for water, sewage and regional parks and has applied to the provincial government to become a full member. Maple Ridge (population 48,422), currently a GVRD member for water and sewer, is considering similar action. Both are currently part of the Dewdney-Alouette Regional District.[18] Two other municipalities – Langley City and Langley Township – joined the GVRD from the Central Fraser Valley Regional District a few years before. Unlike two-tier metropolitan and regional governments in Quebec and Ontario, the GVRD has actually expanded its boundaries since its inception. The fact that peripheral municipalities, prior to their application for full membership, have already been part of the GVRD for a limited number of functions is no doubt part of the explanation.

The fact that the territory of the GVRD is almost congruent with that of the CMA has not prevented serious observers from arguing that it is still far too small. Michael Y. Seelig and Alan F.J. Artibise of the School of Community and Regional Planning at the University of British Columbia (UBC) maintain that "[a] realistic definition of our region should cover a true economic unit."[19] This unit, which they call the Pacific Fraser Region, takes in all or part of six regional districts covering 5,250 square kilometres. It extends from Hope in the Fraser Valley in the east, to the GVRD in the southwest, and north to Whistler

map 3
greater vancouver regional district

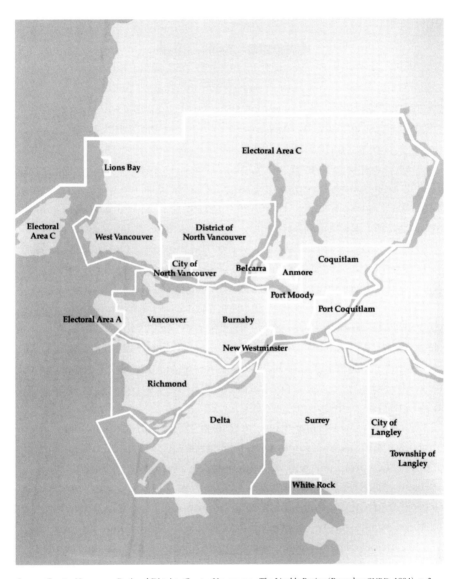

Source: Greater Vancouver Regional District, *Greater Vancouver... The Livable Region* (Burnaby: GVRD, 1994), p. 2.

Mountain and the Sunshine Coast. They claim that such a region "is large enough to encompass the major demographic, social, economic and ecological issues we must face if we are to maintain the quality of life we so cherish."[20] While much larger in territory than the existing GVRD, the population of the Pacific Fraser Region would still only be 1.7 million while that of the GVRD is 1.6 million. But Seelig and Artibise predict a population of 2.7 million for Pacific Fraser by 2010.[21] Such a dramatic projected population increase is what explains their commitment to drastic structural change. Without such change, they argue that unplanned suburban sprawl will engulf the whole area.

While less apocalyptic in approach than Seelig and Artibise, UBC geographers Robert N. North and Walter Hardwick also conclude that "the GVRD is too small an area for adequate planning." But their preferred planning region extends west across the Strait of Georgia. "In the past the waterway between Vancouver and Vancouver Island was generally seen as a barrier. From an industrial point of view, however, it provides efficient, low-cost transportation... The ferry system is already one of the most effective in the world...."[22] Whether such a "Georgia Strait Region" would ever be institutionalized as a regional district or other form of local government is not made clear.

The current GVRD, constrained in territorial terms though it may be, comprises 18 municipalities as full members as well as three unincorporated electoral areas. Its board of directors has 29 members who cast 89 votes. The five members from the City of Vancouver cast 24 votes or 27 percent of the total.[23] Because Vancouver's population of 471,844 is 30.6 percent of that of the GVRD, the city is slightly under-represented.

More so than for any other metropolitan area in Canada, planners in Vancouver are obsessed, for understandable reasons, with protecting the natural physical environment and with maintaining a "liveable region." In the mid-1970s, the GVRD adopted its *Livable Region Plan* (LRP). Its main objective was to prevent urban sprawl by minimizing commuting. More jobs would be created in regional town centres so people could live closer to where they worked.

Recent assessments of the effects of the original LRP contain conflicting conclusions as to its overall effectiveness.[24] In 1990, the GVRD adopted an updated version of the LRP called *Choosing Our Future*. Once again, there are conflicting views about the utility of the document's 54 recommendations. Oberlander and Smith consider it a real achievement to have reached such a regional "policy consensus,"[25] while Ley, Hiebert and Pratt note that "[f]or the cynic, this is merely window dressing – an unobtainable wish list." However, they do acknowledge that

> even as rhetoric, the breadth of the vision of the document gives pause for thought, particularly in a province where the message of the 1980s has been social restraint, privatization, and the often one-dimensional pursuit of economic development.[26]

This passage highlights one of the main features of regional planning in Vancouver: it has usually been seen as a way of limiting economic growth, rather than promoting it. In part, this is because both the LRP and *Choosing Our Future* documents were drafted during times of relative economic prosperity. But it is also because many residents of Vancouver seem profoundly worried that continued economic growth might destroy the remarkable natural environment which makes the area so inherently attractive, or livable. Such worries appear to inject a greater sense of urgency into the regional planning process than in any other Canadian metropolitan area. The GVRD might not have much authority, but its planning activities spark considerable public involvement.

Worrying about the impact of economic growth does not mean that strategies for economic development are irrelevant. Indeed, if the object is to substitute environmentally friendly growth for the kind that consumes agricultural and recreational land while polluting air and water, the need for such strategies seem all the greater. Seelig and Artibise have aptly noted that the *Choosing Our Future* process virtually ignored "the economic transformation of the region, the essential underpinning of any plan for livability."[27] They argue that an independent commission is needed to determine new municipal boundaries in the area as well as expanded boundaries for the regional district.[28] In their view, such steps are necessary to shape Vancouver's future as an innovative urban centre in the world's most economically dynamic region, the Pacific Rim. While their argument about the need for the people of the Vancouver city-region to think as much about advancing and diversifying their economy as about planning and protecting their environment seems indisputable, it is not at all clear that this requires significant changes in municipal structures. Indeed, the provincial government itself is ideally suited both to consult interested parties in the region and to develop strategies to ensure that Vancouver continues its role as a generator of wealth for the entire province.

Assessment

The Regional Municipality of Niagara and the Greater Vancouver Regional District are both upper-tier municipal organizations providing water-supply and sewer systems and the boundaries of both closely coincide with those of their respective census metropolitan areas. In terms of the classification formula adopted for this project, they both are labelled comprehensive two-tier systems. Here the similarities end. Niagara comprises 12 consolidated lower-tier municipalities; since its creation there have been no boundary changes. When the GVRD was created, no municipalities were consolidated but, since then, the GVRD has expanded outward by taking in new members. In Niagara, police, social services and the making of official land-use plans are regional functions; in Vancouver they are not. In Vancouver, air-pollution control, hospital planning, social housing, regional parks and some aspects of solid-waste management are regional functions; in Niagara they are not.

We have already seen that, in the *Financial Times of Canada* survey of municipal efficiency, Vancouver ranked sixth among 11 city-regions surveyed. All those ranked higher have smaller populations. Niagara was not included. Kitchener – with a two-tier system much like that of Niagara and with a population similar in size – was just ahead of Vancouver. In general, comprehensive two-tier systems seem not to be as *efficient* as comprehensive consolidated systems. Perhaps this is because of the duplication caused by having two different levels of municipal government. In any event, in terms of *political accountability,* the Niagara system seems superior to that of the GVRD, primarily because of the existence of regional councillors directly elected to serve only at the regional level. In terms of efficiency potentially caused by the *discipline of the marketplace,* both seem roughly similar although, since fewer high-cost functions are carried out at the regional level in Vancouver, there are more functions for which potential competition can take place among the municipalities. For example, in Vancouver there can be inter-municipal comparisons on police costs, while in Niagara, there cannot.

Comprehensive two-tier systems are ideally structured for *effectiveness.* Precisely because they have two tiers, the upper-tier boundaries can extend far out into the countryside, making possible regional planning for outward urban expansion. To the extent that the upper tier has control over the development of infrastructure, the implementation of regional plans is easier. Niagara and the GVRD both have control over water supply and sewers, and Niagara has jurisdiction over roads that are deemed to serve a regional purpose. In both Niagara and Vancouver, problems have emerged in the development and implementation of formal regional-planning documents. In Vancouver, provincial politicians have eliminated the statutory authority of the GVRD, while in Niagara the problem has been that local politicians have been reluctant to cooperate in implementing declared provincial objectives.

In the final analysis, however, lists of official regional functions or assessments of the legal status of regional planning documents tell us little about the ways in which upper-tier governments actually affect the quality of urban life. For example, it seems quite possible that GVRD planning documents, without legal status, have been more influential than the authoritative official plans in Niagara. Technical differences between the two upper-tier governments are far less significant than the fundamentally different assumptions about municipal government on which they are constructed. Niagara is meant to be a municipal federation in which both tiers are equal in status. From Niagara's perspective, the GVRD is almost unrecognizable as a distinct level of government. The GVRD is best conceptualized as an institution for inter-municipal collaboration. Niagara is itself a municipality.

Assessments of the relative merits of these distinct approaches to two-tier municipal systems will likely be determined by the set of assumptions with which we begin. If we are looking for a distinct upper-tier government for a city-region, directly accountable to the residents, then the Niagara model is clearly superior. If we are looking for a flexible institution designed to assist municipalities in doing things they cannot do themselves, then we will prefer the GVRD.

Notes

1. Ministry of Municipal Affairs, Niagara Region Review Commission, *Report and Recommendations* (Toronto: The Queen's Printer for Ontario, 1989), p. 34.

2. Niagara Review Commission, *Report* (1989), pp. 34-35.

3. Ontario, Ministry of Treasury, Economics and Intergovernmental Affairs, Niagara Region Study Review Commission, *Niagara Region* (1977), chap. 2.

4. Harry Kitchen, *The Role for Local Governments in Economic Development*, Discussion Paper Series (Toronto: Ontario Economic Council, 1985).

5. Donald A. Stewart, *Planning Study for the Regional Municipality of Niagara*, Background Study (Niagara Falls: Niagara Region Review Commission, 1988), p. 7.

6. Niagara Region Review Commission, *Report* (1989), p. 212.

7. Stewart, *Planning Study*, p. 8.

8. Stewart, *Planning Study*, p. 212.

9. Lionel D. Feldman Consulting Ltd., *Public Works in the Niagara Region*, Background Study (Niagara Falls: Niagara Region Review Commission, 1988), p. 25.

10. Niagara Region Review Commission, *Report* (1989), p. 198.

11. Niagara Region Review Commission, *Report* (1989), p.199.

12. Niagara Region Review Commission, *Report* (1989), p. 270.

13. Niagara Region Review Commission, *Report* (1989), p. 232.

14. Niagara Region Review Commission, *Report* (1989), p. 239-40.

15. "Local Economic Development Policy: What Explains the Divergence between Political Analysis and Political Behaviour?", *Journal of Urban Affairs*, Vol. 10, no. 1 (1988), pp. 19-28.

16. H. Peter Oberlander and Patrick J. Smith, "Governing Metropolitan Vancouver: Regional Intergovernmental Relations in British Columbia," in Donald N. Rothblatt and Andrew Sancton (eds.), *Metropolitan Governance: American/Canadian Intergovernmental Perspectives* (Berkeley, CA: Institute of Governmental Studies Press, 1993), pp. 335.

17. Oberlander and Smith, "Governing Metropolitan Vancouver," p. 363.

18. Greater Vancouver Regional District, *News*, January-February, 1993, p. 3.

19. Michael Seelig and Alan Artibise, *From Desolation to Hope: The Pacific Fraser Region in 2010* (Vancouver: Vancouver Board of Trade, 1991), p. 8.

20. Seelig and Artibise, *From Desolation to Hope*, p. 3.

21. Seelig and Artibise, *From Desolation to Hope*, p. 15.

22. "Vancouver Since the Second World War: An Economic Geography," in Graeme Wynn and Timothy Oke (eds.), *Vancouver and Its Region* (Vancouver: UBC Press, 1992), p. 232.

23. GVRD, *News*, January-February, 1993.

24. For a negative view of the LRP's overall effectiveness, see David Ley, Daniel Hiebert and Geraldine Pratt, "Time to grow up? From Urban Village to World City, 1966-91," in Wynn and Oke (eds.), *Vancouver*, pp. 263-64. For a more positive appraisal, see Oberlander and Smith, "Governing Metropolitan Vancouver," p. 364.

25. Oberlander and Smith, "Governing Metropolitan Vancouver," p. 365.

26. Ley, Hiebert and Pratt, "Time to grow up?," p. 264.

27. Seelig and Artibise, *From Desolation to Hope*, p. 72.

28. Seelig and Artibise, *From Desolation to Hope*, p. 93. For a more detailed listing of other possible institutional arrangements, see Alan F.J. Artibise and Jessie Hill, *Governance and Sustainability in the Georgia Basin*, A Background Paper for the British Columbia Round Table on the Environment and the Economy (Victoria: Queen's Printer, 1993), pp. 14-26.

5

Multiple Two-Tier Systems For a Single Metropolitan Area

As demonstrated in the previous chapter, the theory behind two-tier systems of urban government is that the upper tier can plan for the entire built-up metropolitan area. In practice, it is far from easy to determine appropriate boundaries. If they extend too far into the countryside, the system will include rural municipalities having virtually nothing in common with residents of the central city. If they do not extend far enough, then real metropolitan planning becomes impossible. Once the boundaries have been determined, they are often difficult to move. An upper-tier government at the time of its creation might well have appropriate boundaries. But, if urban development takes place for 30 or 40 years without any outward extension of the boundaries, then the upper tier is bound to lose control of its area's overall development.

Non-Comprehensive Two-Tier Systems

Two-tier systems are considered non-comprehensive in this study when they take in less than 90 percent of the entire region's population. On the surface at least, such arrangements appear to have no redeeming features. Despite two tiers of municipal government, there is still no government for the entire area. The Canadian cases are listed in table 5. Quebec City and Ottawa-Carleton are rather anomalous in that in both cases the CMA crosses a significant river but the boundaries of the upper-tier government do not. In Ottawa-Carleton's case the river is also a provincial boundary, creating a set of problems unique among CMAs. The federal presence adds yet another dimension not found elsewhere.[1]

table 5
canadian census metropolitan areas (CMAs)
whose central upper-tier municipalities account for less
than 90 percent of the total population, 1991

CMA	Percent of CMA population in central municipality	Total CMA population
Québec	75.9%	645,550
Ottawa-Hull	73.6%	920,857
Montréal	56.8%	3,127,242
Toronto	53.7%	4,235,756 (GTA)

Source: Statistics Canada, *A National Overview* (Ottawa: Supply and Services Canada), Catalogue no. 93-301

For Montreal and Toronto, the main issues involve the future of the upper-tier governments. What are their roles if their territorial extent is so limited? Is there any prospect of extended boundaries? If not, how can any governmental consensus emerge on economic development issues of concern to the whole city-region?

Toronto

Established in 1953, the Municipality of Metropolitan Toronto is the upper tier of North America's first and best known two-tier system of urban municipal government. In the late 1940s and early 1950s, rural townships surrounding the City of Toronto – especially Etobicoke, North York and Scarborough – were undergoing rapid suburbanization. But they were ill-equipped to provide the necessary services. Some suburban political leaders urged the creation of new inter-municipal bodies to enable the new suburban areas to provide the services themselves. In 1950, the City of Toronto, reversing a 25-year-old policy against annexation, took the position that the best structural solution was for Toronto to absorb the newly urbanized areas within its own expanded boundaries. Employing a line of argument that was to be used again in Winnipeg in 1971 and in London, Ontario in 1992, the city council held that only with municipal consolidation could Toronto "meet the intensive competition from other industrial centres."[2]

In 1950, the Ontario Municipal Board (OMB) began public hearings on the two alternative solutions. In January 1953, its chairman, Lorne Cumming, announced that he was recommending a compromise solution: the creation of a two-tier federated form of municipal government comprising the City of Toronto and 12 surrounding municipalities. A few months later, the Ontario legislature enacted this proposal and on January 1, 1954 the Municipality of Metropolitan Toronto came into being. Its main initial functions were to build new arterial roads and water-supply and sewage systems. Costs were to be paid for by each municipality in proportion to its share of total taxable property assessment within the boundaries of the new "Metro" system. In 1954, this meant that the City of Toronto was paying 62 percent of the cost.[3]

Despite its heavy financial commitment to Metro and despite the fact that it comprised 57 percent of Metro's population,[4] the city was given only 12 of the 24 seats on Metro's governing council. In its early years, there can be little doubt that the main purpose of the Metro system was to use the city's resources to finance new infrastructure in the suburbs. In this respect it was remarkably successful.

By 1963, the city's shares of Metro's taxable property assessment and population had declined to 44 percent and 38 percent respectively,[5] but it still held half the seats on Metro council. Greater violations of the principle of representation by population could be found among the suburbs. North York, with a population of 308,000, was still allocated only one seat; so was Swansea with its population of 9,000.[6] In the same year, Premier John Robarts appointed H. Carl Goldenberg of Montreal to review the entire Metro system. In 1965, the Goldenberg commission recommended that the 13 municipalities be consolidated into four and that each be represented on the Metro council in proportion to its population. In 1966, much of the report was implemented, except that six consolidated municipalities were created instead of four.[7]

In light of subsequent developments, it is important to realize that the Goldenberg commission did investigate the possible outward expansion of Metro's boundaries. It noted that, between 1953 and 1963, the population of 13 "fringe" municipalities outside Metro grew by 96 percent while the population increase within Metro was only 40 percent.[8] After a careful analysis of the relevant considerations, the commission concluded that the boundaries should not be extended. Instead, it recommended that the province and/or Metro provide water and sewer services to urbanized areas of York County on Metro's northern boundaries, that Metro's planning authority outside its boundaries be extended, and that further consideration be given to "municipal reorganization in the fringe areas."[9] By 1974, Metro services had been extended northward and the fringe areas had been reorganized as the regional municipalities of Halton, Peel, York and Durham. Metro's extra-territorial planning authority had been transferred to the new regional governments[10] and Metro's original boundaries, which were described in the Cumming Report of 1953 as "temporary,"[11] had become sacrosanct.

The most important structural change within Metro since 1966 was the reorganization of Metro council in 1988. In 1977, a royal commission headed by the former Ontario Premier, John Robarts, recommended a council composed of the mayors of the six constituent municipalities and 27 councillors directly elected from specially designated Metro wards. Each of the 27 Metro councillors would also sit on the local council of his or her respective lower-tier municipality.[12] As a result of yet another study on the same issue in 1986,[13] the direct election of 28 Metro councillors was implemented in 1988. Under this scheme, local mayors still sit on Metro council but Metro councillors have no role on lower-tier councils.[14]

Another important development in 1988 was the creation by the provincial government of the Office of the Greater Toronto Area (OGTA). Although it reports to a cabinet minister with other responsibilities, the small OGTA staff is headed by a deputy minister, indicating that it is supposed to have considerable importance within the provincial bureaucracy. Its main objective is to bring together those parts of the government whose work directly affects the wider Toronto area in order to solve immediate inter-agency problems and to develop a broad consensus on government policy concerning longer-term issues.[15]

The OGTA acts as a secretariat for the Greater Toronto Co-ordinating Committee (GTCC), which includes a senior staff representative from all upper-and lower-tier municipalities within the Greater Toronto Area (GTA): Metropolitan Toronto, Halton, Peel, York and Durham.[16] Among the 30 lower-tier municipalities, the City of Toronto (1991 population of 635,395) is the largest, but North York (562,564), Scarborough (524,598) and Mississauga (463,388) are not far behind.

In November 1991, the OGTA established a "working group" on economic vitality chaired by the OGTA's assistant deputy minister. It comprised 15 other members: six senior employees of GTA municipalities and nine provincial

map 4
the toronto metropolitan area:
alternative boundary definitions

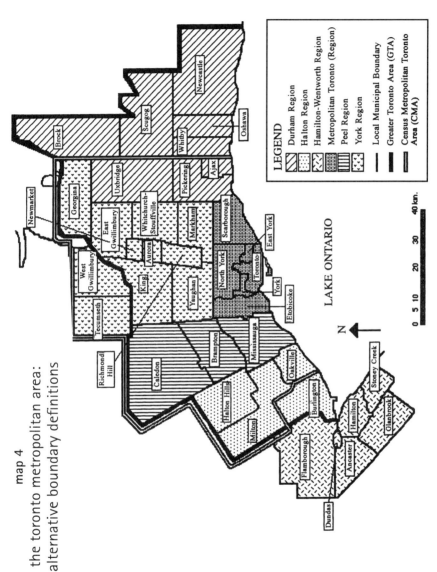

LEGEND

- Durham Region
- Halton Region
- Hamilton-Wentworth Region
- Metropolitan Toronto (Region)
- Peel Region
- York Region

— Local Municipal Boundary
— Greater Toronto Area (GTA)
— Census Metropolitan Toronto Area (CMA)

LAKE ONTARIO

N

0 5 10   20   30   40 km.

Source: D.N. Rothblatt and A. Sancton (eds.), *Metropolitan Governance: American/Canadian Intergovernmental Perspectives* (Berkeley, CA: Institute of Governmental Studies Press, 1993), p.156.

public servants, each from a different ministry. The working group's report concluded that:

> The GTAs [sic] role and dynamics present significant challenges and possible risks in the creation of an economic strategy. For this reason, the group's work suggests the elements of a strategy, without stating an actual plan of action or critical path. In general, however, the findings of the working group point to the need to attract knowledge-based, value added industries.[17]

How could such a laudable objective be achieved? The working group listed seven "possible actions," none of which is in any sense original or especially tailored to the particular circumstances of the GTA. One of the possible actions was this: "priority should be given to integrated infrastructure planning and investment."[18] Unfortunately, there was no suggestion as to how such integration could take place.

Another working group did address this issue. Chaired by the Director of the Municipal Finance Branch in the Ministry of Municipal Affairs and comprising 11 other financial and policy-planning officials from four provincial ministries, five municipalities and the Metropolitan Toronto Board of Education, the group was charged with recommending new mechanisms for integrated investment planning and financing. Its report emphasized the fact that many municipal capital projects in a multi-municipal metropolitan area have important implications for neighbouring jurisdictions and should therefore be subject to some form of joint decision making. The working group suggested four important questions that should be asked to determine the appropriateness of joint decision making:

- will economies of scale be achieved for facilities beyond the size appropriate for regional municipalities;

- are strategic links (e.g., regional roads) that cross municipal boundaries involved;

- do other factors, which are not related to political boundaries, more appropriately dictate infrastructure placement; and

- are there spillovers, i.e., do businesses and people in one municipal-ity depend on the infrastructure in another municipality? Or, simi-larly, are such people and businesses otherwise affected by the infra-structure choices of neighbouring municipalities?[19]

After reviewing the structure of 14 different "inter-regional decision-mak-ing bodies" in Canada, the US, Britain, Ireland and Japan, the group "developed three new decision-making models, which could apply in the GTA." The first was a "Joint Review Committee" comprising the "Heads of Council and select-ed ministries." It would review the investment plans of all public bodies in the GTA and make recommendations to improve integration. However, participa-tion would be voluntary and the committee's role would be purely advisory.[20]

The second alternative was to establish a "Special-Purpose Body" which would have "full authority to make decisions for a specific infrastructure type." Members would be appointed by, and accountable to, the provincial cabinet. Apart from reducing municipal autonomy and authority, the main perceived problem with this arrangement was that there would be "no incentive to weigh competing priorities" among different special-purpose bodies.[21]

The working group's "preferred model" was a "Supra Body" comprising "municipal elected officials at the regional level." It would have "full authority" over roads, transit, sewers, water and waste "to decide which investments are made, when and where they are built, how they are financed and who pays." The main problems with such a new body are that it would be "[p]erceived as a new level of government"; it would involve a "[l]oss of autonomy for regional governments"; and it "presents some accountability issues."[22]

A commentary on the working group reports was prepared for the OGTA by a consulting company and published in September 1992. The consultants had this to say about possible changes in local-government structures:

[F]rom the beginning of the process to establish a growth manage-ment strategy for the GTA, the Province has insisted that it was pre-mature to discuss restructuring of governance arrangements. Their rationale was and continues to be that any debate around the issue would be so time consuming and pervasive that the issues of growth management and planning would be overshadowed for several years.

In fact, good planning techniques dictate that the issues be addressed first. The structure needed to implement the solutions will then become clearer and may require little change from the present structure. The Province's policy has accordingly been to work with the existing 35 municipalities to develop a growth management strategy. It is clear that the province intends to continue with this cooperative approach.[23]

The approach the province has chosen might well be the most appropriate in the circumstances. But it was not the approach taken in the early 1950s for Toronto or for other rapidly urbanizing parts of the province in the late 1960s and early 1970s. Nor was it the approach taken in London, Ontario. At the same time as the government was promoting inter-municipal cooperation in Toronto, it was legislating London's massive annexation on the grounds that, without major boundary changes, opportunities for economic growth would be lost. Nowhere has the Ontario government explained why structural reform was needed in London but not in the GTA.

One is left to conclude that the creation of five two-tier systems of municipal government in the area covered by the GTA was a mistake but that, since the most recent is only twenty years old, it is too soon to scrap them and start again. The result is that, although all the territory covered by the GTA has been municipally re-organized in a fashion not experienced in any other major Canadian metropolitan area, the only way to integrate their activities is through provincial leadership and voluntary inter-municipal cooperation.

Montreal[24]

The Island of Montreal's upper-tier government – the Montreal Urban Community (MUC) came into existence in 1970.[25] Unlike the origins of Metro Toronto, the creation of the MUC had nothing to do with problems of regional planning and suburban development. There was indeed a service crisis in Montreal in 1969, but it was in the central city, not the suburbs. By the late 1960s, Montreal's well-known mayor, Jean Drapeau, had exhausted the city's financial resources through various grandiose schemes, most notably an unusually luxurious subway system and the 1967 World Exhibition. Meanwhile, street demonstrations and terrorist activities in support of an independent, French-speaking and socialist Quebec had placed enormous strains on Montreal's municipal police department. In October 1969 the police went on strike, their declared objective being to receive salaries equal to those paid in Metro Toronto.

Although the strike lasted only 16 hours, its destructive impact in the downtown area was devastating. Suburban municipalities, especially those close to downtown Montreal, successfully deployed their own independent police forces around their borders to defend against vandals and armed robbers. In the immediate aftermath of the strike, the city administration convinced a frightened provincial government that, notwithstanding Montreal's inability to pay, the police should receive a substantial pay increase. The suburbs were identified as the main potential revenue sources and the MUC was devised as the mechanism for effecting the transfer of funds.

In structural terms, the MUC was designed to be the City of Montreal writ large. Its council consists of the entire membership of the city council (now 59) plus the mayors (now 27) of all the Island suburbs, including one small municipality on a separate island northwest of the main one. In addition, the person chosen by the council to be chairman of the executive committee is also an MUC council member even though he or she must resign other municipal positions upon taking office. Total membership of the council is 87. Each city member casts as many votes as there are thousands of people in the city divided by 59. Each mayor casts as many votes as there are thousands of people in his or her municipality. Prior to 1982, motions were not deemed to be approved in the MUC council unless they were approved by a double majority of both city and suburban members. Since 1982, the double majority refers to both city and suburban votes, not members.

As in the City of Montreal, most of the real authority rests with the executive committee. Prior to 1982, the MUC executive committee comprised the city executive committee of seven members plus five suburban representatives. Since 1982, it has been made up of six suburban representatives, six city representatives, and the chairman. The chairman does not have a particularly powerful decision-making role because executive-committee decisions require the assent of at least four of both the city and suburban representatives. Elaborate mechanisms are in place for executive-committee deadlocks to be eventually determined by the council.

The MUC came into being with an impressive list of potential functions but, in the early years at least, most of its political controversies related primarily to the implementation of a provincial-government decision to create a single

MUC police department to serve the whole Island. The main effect of this decision was to redistribute significant financial resources from the suburbs to the central city. For many in the suburbs, the MUC continues to be viewed as the institution responsible for eliminating the locally controlled police force and causing massive increases in property taxes.

In 1971, the MUC population of 1.959 million accounted for 71 percent of the 1971 census metropolitan area. By 1991, MUC population had slipped to 1.775 million, comprising only 57 percent of the 1991 metropolitan area. These numbers tell us not only that the metropolitan government is becoming relatively less important within the entire metropolitan area, but also that it is simply not present where most of the new development is taking place: the outer suburbs.

The drawing of the original MUC boundaries was not difficult. The existence of the Island of Montreal presented provincial policy makers with a relatively easy option: make the boundaries of the metropolitan government correspond to that of the Island and two small adjoining islands (Bizard and Dorval), each of which was municipally incorporated. Such boundaries encapsulated most of the east-west axis of urban development, but were woefully deficient for the north-south.

From the very beginning of the MUC, the underground rapid-transit system (the Métro) served Longueuil, an important municipality across the St. Lawrence River to the south. Until 1985, Longueuil was considered, for transit purposes only, as an MUC member. Starting in 1989, a regional transit coordinating agency — the *Conseil métropolitain de transport en commun* (CMTC) – has been in place to bring together representatives of the MUC transit system (STCUM), the south shore system (STRSM), and that of the City of Laval (STL), which occupies a large island immediately to the north of the Island of Montreal. In setting up the agency, the provincial government spread financial responsibility for subway operating deficits and for previous municipal capital borrowing among all municipalities served by the three systems. The new agency is responsible for transit coordination, fare integration and system planning. But Frances Frisken has concluded that

> Because that organization's jurisdiction is limited to the territory served by the three largest operators ... it lacks both the authority and the membership to influence transit decisions in the rapidly developing outer municipalities or to integrate them into an effective regional system.[26]

On the basis of a policy first proposed in 1978, the provincial government committed itself to preventing extensive peripheral suburban development.[27] Instead, it aimed to bolster the MUC's position as the dominant centre of the Montreal metropolitan area. The main object of the policy was to avoid costly investment in new outer-suburban infrastructure at a time when many MUC facilities (especially the major sewage-treatment plant) still had surplus capacity. By 1983, the policy had become known as "L'Option préférable" and was being enforced with varying degrees of severity on various peripheral local governments in the Montreal area.[28]

In the early 1980s, as result of the passage in 1979 of the province's first comprehensive land-use planning law, municipal government in the peripheral areas was significantly re-organized. Prior to 1979, the MUC and the City of Laval were surrounded by dozens of single-tier cities and towns and a handful of traditional two-tier counties comprising villages and parishes. The new law called for the creation of "municipalités régionales de comté" (MRCs), the main function of which was to adopt a development plan covering both urban and rural areas.[29] Boundaries of existing municipalities were not threatened; MRC boundaries were worked out as a result of a process of local negotiation. A combination of provincial financial incentives and tough regulations ensured that all affected municipalities eventually complied.

The end result for the census metropolitan area of Montreal (as it existed in 1991) was that 102 municipalities were organized into one urban community (the MUC) and thirteen MRCs, two of which comprised only a single municipality (Laval and Mirabel). Of the 11 multi-member MRCs, five are entirely within the census metropolitan area and six are not. The upper-tier municipal components of the census metropolitan area are shown in table 6.

By creating the MRCs in the early 1980s, the Quebec government seemed to be specifically rejecting the option of extending the boundaries of the Montreal Urban Community. Given that no one favoured extending the territory of the MUC police force or the scope of the MUC sewer system (beyond Laval at least), it is hardly surprising that MUC expansion was never an issue. Furthermore, the creation of the new public-transit coordinating agency in 1989 meant that any potential arguments for MUC expansion for public-transit purposes had lost much of their force.

The strongest potential case for MUC territorial expansion could in theory be based on the need for metropolitan-wide planning. What is significant here, however, is that ever since 1977 it has been apparent that the provincial government

map 5
montreal census metropolitan area, 1971 and 1991

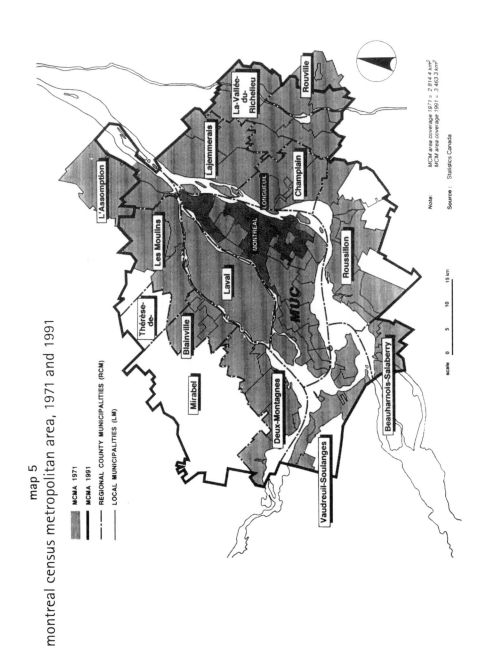

▨ MCMA 1971
▬ MCMA 1991
–·– REGIONAL COUNTY MUNICIPALITIES (RCM)
— LOCAL MUNICIPALITIES (LM)

Note: MCM area coverage 1971 = 2 814.4 km²
           MCM area coverage 1991 = 3 463.3 km²

Source :   Statistics Canada

scale   0   5   10   15 km

table 6
upper-tier municipal components of the census metropolitan area of montreal

Name	Number of lower-tier units	Population
Montreal Urban Community	29	1,775,871
Ville de Laval	1	314,398
MRC Champlain	6	312,734
MRC Rousillon	11	118,355
MRC Thérèse-de-Blainville	7	104,693
MRC La Vallée-du-Richelieu (part)	9	97,794
MRC Les Moulins	4	91,156
MRC Lajemmerais (part)	4	74,990
MRC L'Assomption (part)	4	71,591
MRC Deux-Montagnes	9	71,218
MRC Vaudreuil-Soulanges (part)	11	57,519
Ville de Mirabel	1	17,971
MRC Beauharnois-Salaberry (part)	3	11,172
MRC Rouville (part)	3	7,780
TOTALS	102	3,127,242

Note: Excludes the populations of Indian reserves at Kahnawake and Kanesatake, which are not municipally organized.
Source: Statistics Canada, *Census Divisions and Census Subdivisions,* 1991 Census of Canada (Ottawa: Supply and Services Canada, 1992), Catalogue number 93-304, pp. 30-60.

has been in charge of this function. The MUC and the MRCs are not themselves able to create any kind of plan for metropolitan Montreal as a whole.[30] Rather, they are the political and administrative mechanisms through which provincial planning policies for the area are to be implemented.

It would be a mistake to assume that the provincial government as a whole has a common policy for metropolitan Montreal. The desire to consolidate urban development within the MUC and to limit peripheral urban sprawl is clearly the priority of the land-use planning interests within the Ministry of Municipal Affairs, and probably the Ministry of the Environment as well. On the other hand, the Ministry of Transport, with the enthusiastic support of the outer suburbs and their political representatives, has been proclaiming the need for what is effectively a new outer-ring road, particularly for the southern part of the area. While there is undoubtedly lots of empirical evidence to support the case for building such new roads, the transportation experts tend to overlook the inevitable strong pressures they would generate for still more peripheral development.

In 1990, the provincial government established a *Comité ministériel permanent de développement du Grand Montréal* (CMPDGM) with "the overall task of promoting the revival of Montreal's economy."[31] Greater Montreal was defined for the committee's purposes as including the MUC and *all* the component municipalities of any MRC completely or partially within the boundaries of the Montreal CMA. "Grand Montréal" is therefore bigger than the CMA. Its 1991 population was 3.233 million and comprised 136 lower-tier municipalities.[32]

In 1991, the committee of eight provincial cabinet ministers, chaired by the president of the Treasury Board, Daniel Johnson, released a report proposing a four-point strategy focussing on the needs for "technological innovation, the modernization of industrial infrastructures, worker training and support for economic development."[33] In discussing the various barriers to Montreal's revitalization, the committee stated that "[t]erritorial organization in Greater Montreal is no longer suited to economic conditions which are those of a major urban centre whose various components are inextricably linked."[34] This finding was one factor causing the Minister of Municipal Affairs in April 1992 to create a 12-person Task Force on Montreal and its Region, one of the main objects of which was to make recommendations for possible changes in the municipal organization of the territory covered by the ministerial committee.[35]

Members of the task force – none of whom were municipal politicians or employees – presented their final report in December 1993. Their main recommendation was that the province establish a Montreal Metropolitan Region, the territory of which would correspond exactly with that of the CMA and which would automatically be adjusted to match future CMA boundary changes. The council of the Region would comprise 21 members, of whom three would be the mayors of Montreal, Laval and Longueuil. Montreal and Laval would also have some municipal councillors as members so as to reflect the principle of representation by population. The remaining members would be mayors of the remaining 99 municipalities as chosen by such mayors.[36]

The main functions of the Region would be: the creation of a regional land-use plan with which all local land-use plans would have to comply; the planning of regional parks; economic development; the enactment of air-quality and sewage-discharge standards; the planning and coordination of roads, public-transit systems and public-transit fares; planning for and subsidizing cultural and artistic facilities and organizations; planning and coordinating specialized police services; preparing emergency measures plans; and coordinating the 911 emergency-call service throughout the region.[37]

The new system would involve abolishing the MRCs created only a decade ago and transforming the MUC into the Intermunicipal Service Agency (ISA) of Montreal. ISAs would also be created for 25 municipalities (excluding Laval) to the north of Montreal, 29 (including Longueuil) to the southeast, and 18 to the southwest. The ISAs would be legal entities with the authority to borrow money but they would have no jurisdiction unless an enabling motion was approved by a two-thirds majority of votes on the ISA Assembly of Mayors. The mayors' votes would be weighted in accordance with the populations of their respective municipalities. ISAs could perform other inter-municipal functions as agreed by particular municipalities but only the affected municipalities would participate in the decision making and financing for those functions.[38]

The ISA of Montreal would be responsible for MUC functions not assigned to the Region. Its governing body would comprise the 29 mayors and nine additional representatives from the City of Montreal. Votes would be weighted in accordance with population. The "double-majority" system currently used within the MUC to protect suburban interests would be retained.[39]

The task force refused to make specific proposals for municipal mergers. Its position was that the creation of the Region and the ISAs were the top priorities for the city-region as a whole. The task force stated that it "understands that there are too many small municipalities in the region and that some municipal coalitions are necessary."[40] It recommended that the ISAs be obligated within two years to make "concrete proposals" to the provincial government for mergers within their respective territories.[41] The task force made no recommendation of its own concerning the minimum population for a municipality, nor did it suggest any practical benefits that would result from municipal mergers. It also failed to note that, although the original legislation establishing the MUC required the Community to establish a plan for municipal boundary restructuring within five years of its creation, no such plan was ever agreed to.[42]

As is the case when any major independent report is released, it is impossible to know if and when the main features of the task force's report will be implemented. Nevertheless, it is clear that a major debate has already been launched in Montreal concerning the governance of the whole city-region. Much of it will likely revolve around concerns that a three-tier system of local government is being proposed for Montreal and that such a system is too unwieldy and complicated. In any event, some form of structural change now seems inevitable. No one is pretending any longer that previous structural reforms created a satisfactory system.

Assessment

Both the Municipality of Metropolitan Toronto and the Montreal Urban Community were originally designed as governments capable of shaping the development of the entire metropolitan area. Given their respective territories, this expectation was much more realistic for Metro in 1954 than it was for the MUC in 1970. But in 1994 it is equally unrealistic for both. In the city-regions of both Montreal and Toronto there are now multiple two-tier systems. Nowhere is there a report or a study advocating such a system. In both city-regions, the systems emerged as one municipal reorganization was added to another. It is impossible to see how the current systems of municipal government can be defended, either on grounds of efficiency or effectiveness.

Quebec City, Ottawa, Toronto and Montreal are the four city-regions in Canada having multiple two-tier systems. In the *Financial Times of Canada* survey of municipal efficiency, the central cities of these regions (all of Metro in the case of Toronto) were ranked eighth, ninth, tenth and eleventh respectively out of 11 city-regions studied.[43] It is easy to think of reasons why services in these cities would be more costly to provide than in others and perhaps their rankings should not be taken too seriously. The fact remains, however, that on the basis of the very limited data available, these central cities do not do well. In Metro Toronto, because of the direct election of Metro councillors, the lines of *political accountability* are now theoretically clearer than in any of the other systems. But this assumes that voters in Metro are perfectly clear about who does what and how the two-tier system works – an assumption that seems dubious at best.

Perhaps there is a form of *discipline of the marketplace* in these systems, but it is difficult to discern within the organizational complexity of the two tiers. In Montreal, the MUC police force is so large compared to the others that meaningful comparisons are not possible. In the GTA, the existence of five regional police forces hardly promotes the kind of competition and diversity suggested by public-choice advocates. An interesting test of the public-choice hypothesis would be to compare total per-capita costs on a lower-tier function (parks and recreation, for example) within the thirty GTA municipalities, the 102 Montreal municipalities, and within major city-regions such as Winnipeg or Calgary, where there is only a single provider of the service in question.

In terms of *potential effectiveness,* it is simply impossible to understand how multiple two-tier systems can be seen to have merit. Despite the two tiers, there is no level of government concerned with the city-region as a whole. The difference between Montreal and Toronto is that, for the former, the Quebec government has at least seriously investigated the problem. In Toronto, it is being discussed in municipal councils and in newspapers, but the provincial government has yet to acknowledge the existence of a problem.[44]

Notes

1. Katherine A. Graham, "Capital Planning/Capital Budgeting: The Future of Canada's Capital," in Frances Abele (ed.), *How Ottawa Spends: The Politics of Competitiveness, 1992-93* (Ottawa: Carleton University Press, 1992), pp. 125-50.

2. Minutes of the Toronto City Council, as quoted in Timothy J. Colton, *Big Daddy: Frederick G. Gardiner and the Building of Metropolitan Toronto* (Toronto: University of Toronto Press, 1980), p. 65.

3. Ontario, *Report of the Royal Commission on Metropolitan Toronto* (1965), p. 79.

4. Ontario, *Report...on Metropolitan Toronto* (1965), p. 11.

5. Ontario, *Report...on Metropolitan Toronto* (1965), pp. 78 and 11.

6. Ontario, *Report...on Metropolitan Toronto* (1965), p. 11.

7. Albert Rose, *Governing Metropolitan Toronto: A Social and Political Analysis, 1953-1971* (Berkeley, CA: University of California Press, 1972), chap. 7.

8. Ontario, *Report...on Metropolitan Toronto* (1965), p. 158.

9. Ontario, *Report...on Metropolitan Toronto* (1965), pp. 170-71.

10. Ontario, *Report of the Royal Commission on Metropolitan Toronto, Vol.2, Detailed Findings and Recommendations* (1977), p. 212.

11. Quoted in Ontario, *Report...on Metropolitan Toronto* (1965), p. 157.

12. Ontario, *Report...on Metropolitan Toronto*, Vol. 2 (1977), p. 88.

13. Ontario, Ministry of Municipal Affairs, Task Force on Representation and Accountability in Metropolitan Toronto, *Analysis and Options for the Government of Metropolitan Toronto* (1986).

14. Hugh Mellon, "Reforming the Electoral System of Metropolitan Toronto: Doing Away with Dual Representation," *Canadian Public Administration*, Vol. 36, no. 1 (Spring 1993), pp. 38-56.

15. Frances Frisken, "Planning and Servicing the Greater Toronto Area: The Interplay of Provincial and Municipal Interests," in Donald N. Rothblatt and Andrew Sancton (eds.), *Metropolitan Governance: American/Canadian Intergovernmental Perspectives* (Berkeley, CA: Institute of Governmental Studies Press, 1993), p. 161.

16. Berridge Lewinberg Greenberg Ltd., *Shaping Growth in the GTA* (Toronto: Office for the Greater Toronto Area, 1992), p. 3.

17. Office of the Greater Toronto Area, Provincial-Municipal Economic Vitality Working Group, *Sustainable Economic Growth* (1992), p. 28.

18. Provincial-Municipal Economic Vitality Working Group, p. 28.

19. Office of the Greater Toronto Area, Provincial-Municipal Investment Planning and Financing Mechanism Working Group, *Meeting the Challenge* (1992), p. 8.

20. Provincial-Municipal Investment Planning, p. 12.

21. Provincial-Municipal Investment Planning, p. 13.

22. Provincial-Municipal Investment Planning, pp. 13-14.

23. Berridge Lewinberg Greenberg Ltd., *Shaping Growth in the GTA*, p. 52.

24. Portions of this section were first written for a paper called "Metropolitan Government in Montreal," scheduled to appear in *The Government of World Cities*, a collection of original essays edited by L.J. Sharpe to be published by Belhaven Press.

25. For a discussion of the creation of the MUC and of its activities from 1970-82, see Andrew Sancton, *Governing the Island of Montreal: Language Differences and Metropolitan Politics* (Berkeley, CA: University of California Press, 1983), chaps. 6 and 7.

26. Frances Frisken, "Provincial Transit Policymaking in the Toronto, Montreal, and Vancouver Regions" in Frances Frisken (ed.), *The Changing Canadian Metropolis: A Public Policy Perspective*, Vol. 2 (Berkeley, CA: Institute of Governmental Studies Press, 1994), p. 532.

27. Marie-Odile Trépanier, "Metropolitan Government in the Montreal Area" in Rothblatt and Sancton (eds.), *Metropolitan Governance*, p. 83.

28. François Charbonneau, Pierre Hamel, and Michel Barcelo, "Urban Sprawl in the Montreal Area – Policies and Trends" in Frisken (ed.), *The Changing Canadian Metropolis*, Vol. 2, p. 469.

29. Louise Quesnel, "Political Control over Planning in Quebec," *International Journal of Urban and Regional Research*, Vol. 14, no. 1 (March 1990), pp. 25-48.

30. The MUC approved its first Development Plan for its own territory in 1987. See Communauté urbaine de Montréal, Service de la planification du territoire, *Development Plan, August 1986* and *Development Plan, Modifications: August 1987, December 1987; Coming into Force December 31, 1987.*

31. Québec, Ministère du Conseil exécutif, Comité ministériel permanent de développement du Grand Montréal, *Change Today for Tomorrow: A Strategic Plan for Greater Montreal* (1991), p. 2.

32. Québec, Ministère des affaires municipales, Task Force on Greater Montreal, *Progress Report* (January 1993), p. A-6.

33. Québec, Comité ministériel, *Change Today*, p. vii.

34. Québec, Comité ministériel, *Change Today*, p. 21

35. Trépanier, "Metropolitan Government in the Montreal Area," p. 89.

36. Québec, Task Force on Greater Montreal, *Montreal: A City-Region* (December 1993), p. 17.

37. Québec, Task Force on Greater Montreal, *Montreal: A City-Region*, p. 23.

38. Québec, Task Force on Greater Montreal, *Montreal: A City-Region*, pp. 19-21.

39. Québec, Task Force on Greater Montreal, *Montreal: A City-Region*, pp. 22 and 24.

40. Québec, Task Force on Greater Montreal, *Montreal: A City-Region*, p. 24.

41. Québec, Task Force on Greater Montreal, *Montreal: A City-Region*, p. 26.

42. Sancton, *Governing the Island*, p. 139.

43. Mark Stevenson, "Where Taxpayers Get the Most for Their Money," *The Financial Times of Canada*, November 7, 1992, p. 11.

44. The recent report of the Sewell commission concerning Ontario's land-use planning system has received considerable public attention. However, the commission itself acknowledges that it did "not have a mandate to address the restructuring of municipal government, and thus it must look to existing structures to perform these functions" (p. 61). The functions referred to are those required for "broad planning." See Ontario, Commission on Planning and Development Reform in Ontario, *Final Report: New Planning for Ontario* (Toronto: Queen's Printer, 1993), p. 61.

Governing Canada's City-Regions: A Look to the Future

During the 1960s and early 1970s, Canadian city-regions were subjected to great changes in their systems of local government. These changes were supposed to improve the quality of our urban life by facilitating the planning of outward expansion, capturing economies of scale and reducing inequities in service levels and tax burdens. To the extent that the new structures forced people in wealthy enclave municipalities to start paying their fare share of costs, they have at least been successful in reducing inequities. But the other alleged gains from structural changes have been elusive at best. Many of their strengths and weaknesses – especially as they relate to local economic development – have been explored in previous chapters. What follows in this concluding chapter is an outline of three of the central lessons that have emerged.

Multiple Two-Tier Systems Serve No Useful Purpose

Neither Montreal nor Toronto has a comprehensive upper-tier level of municipal government. Greater Montreal has one relatively strong upper-tier government (the MUC) and a number of weak ones (the MRCs). The Greater Toronto Area has one metropolitan government and four strong regional governments. There is no possible justification for such a state of affairs. Both Montreal and Toronto must live with all the disadvantages of two-tier systems (inefficiencies caused by duplication, overlap, conflict) while still having no one local government capable of effectively dealing with issues affecting the city-region as a whole.

It is relatively easy to point out the problem but much more difficult to suggest remedies. The Task Force on Greater Montreal has made a valiant effort but has come perilously close to recommending a *three*-tier system of local government. By limiting the functions of the proposed new agency for the whole city-region and by downgrading the MUC to an inter-municipal service-provision agency, the task force has attempted to avoid the three-tier label. But if or how it will ever be made to work in practice remains to be seen.

The provincial Office of the Greater Toronto Area has so far carefully avoided issues relating to municipal structures. But sooner or later these will have to be faced. There are three alternatives. The first is to maintain the *status quo,* but with a possible strengthening of the Greater Toronto Coordinating Committee. Such an approach would be similar to that recommended by the Task Force on Greater Montreal. The problem here, as in Montreal, is the subtle introduction of a third level of local government at a time when the popular view is that institutions of government need to be streamlined, not made more complicated.

A second alternative is to consolidate all municipalities within each of the five two-tier systems. A new upper-tier planning and infrastructure authority could then be created for the whole GTA. This plan seems logical in principle but provokes a number of potentially difficult questions. Would inner-city residential areas in Toronto survive in a municipal system dominated by commuters in North York, Scarborough and Etobicoke? Would there be anything local about municipal governments stretching from Steeles Avenue to Lake Simcoe (York), from Lake Ontario to Lake Simcoe (Durham), from Mississauga to Caledon (Peel) or from Burlington to Acton (Halton)? Is there any evidence that such huge authorities would be more effective and efficient, especially given the wide variations in the kinds of residents they would be expected to serve?

The third alternative is to abolish the five existing upper-tier governments and replace them with a single new one. The new two-tier system would then contain thirty lower-tier municipalities. The main problem with this solution is figuring out what to do with services currently provided by the existing upper-tier units – services that might not be appropriate for a new authority covering the entire GTA. The most obvious problems are policing and social services. All the same, as long as municipal police forces in Ontario remain under the control of police services boards rather than municipal governments, there is no need to change their territorial jurisdictions. Police services boards can continue to be made up in exactly the same way as they are now.

The future of municipal social services in Ontario has been in question for many years. It seems entirely possible to pass General Welfare Assistance on to the province, to have the new GTA authority responsible for social-service planning and to place some operational functions (old-age homes, seniors' services and child care) with the lower-tier municipalities or with new special-purpose bodies.

New upper-tier authorities for Greater Montreal or for the GTA would not simply be Metro Toronto or the MUC writ large. Their territories would be larger but their political structures and their staffs would be less elaborate and more flexible. Greater Vancouver can provide the model. It will be reviewed in the final pages of this chapter.

Municipal Consolidation Is Not the Answer

At a time when Canadians are searching for cheaper, more efficient government as a means of improving their overall economic situation, it is not surprising that some are advocating fewer governments. Since the one federal, ten provincial and two (soon to be three) territorial governments are unlikely to be consolidated, people's attention inevitably turns to the hundreds of local governments in Canada. Many of these local governments are special-purpose bodies concerned with such matters as public education and policing. To the extent that such bodies share common boundaries with municipalities, there is a good case for consolidation, although constitutional difficulties emerge in the field of education.

A better known form of local-government consolidation involves joining together two or more contiguous municipalities or school boards. In chapter 2, we reviewed debates concerning such municipal consolidations in Winnipeg and in London, Ontario. In chapter 3, reference was made to attempted consolidations in Halifax and Edmonton. In each case the proposal caused great local controversy but its fate was settled in the provincial arena. British Columbia is the one Canadian jurisdiction in which changes to municipal boundaries are always decided by local residents through referenda, but there have been no recent examples in which significant changes have been approved. In Quebec there have been two recent cases of consolidation (in Lévis and Sorel) to which the relevant local councils consented. A proposal to amalgamate Gatineau, Hull and Aylmer was defeated in a local referendum conducted in 1990.[1]

Municipal consolidations that are approved by the affected local residents need hardly be questioned. In particular circumstances, there might also be powerful cases for consolidation – for example, if a municipality is not financially viable or if there are glaring inequities among contiguous municipalities. But the most common justification for consolidation is that it will reduce costs, thereby making the municipal system as a whole more efficient. The problem with such a justification is that there is no empirical evidence to support it.

Data from the *Financial Times of Canada* survey suggests that one-tier systems are more efficient than two-tier systems but, since there were no examples of non-comprehensive single-tier systems, we cannot arrive at any conclusions concerning the virtues of consolidation within a single-tier system. Likewise, there is no evidence to suggest that there would be efficiency gains from lower-tier consolidations within a two-tier system, such as that of Metro Toronto. The fact that the Task Force on Greater Montreal, when confronted with 136 municipalities within its territorial frame of reference, was unwilling or unable to recommend any criteria for municipal consolidations is highly significant.

If we begin to think of municipalities more as "arrangers" of services, rather than as direct providers, many of the points in dispute about municipal consolidation become irrelevant. We can begin again to conceptualize municipalities as the political expression of territorial communities. There might still be local disputes about which territory belongs where, but they could be worked out by local people on the basis of local conceptions of community rather than on expert advice about the imperatives of certain municipal services. Allowing local communities to define their own municipal territories does not imply that they can then do whatever they want – such as exclude poor people. There would still be many circumstances in which provincial regulation of municipal practices would be fully justified.

City-Regions Need a Regional Institution

Can a large city-region contain a number of municipalities, establish a regional local-government institution and avoid the pitfalls of two-tier municipal government? This is the biggest structural question facing urban government today. While strict adherents to the public-choice approach might still reject the need for any form of metropolitan or regional government, their views are now not likely to be accepted even by those most interested in making government more entrepreneurial. For example, after a very brief survey of "regional government" issues in the US, David Osborne and Ted Gaebler vaguely conclude that "most areas are under pressure to find some way to get their hands around the new problems of the metropolitan region."[2]

It is not at all clear exactly what Osborne and Gaebler have in mind but it seems quite likely that the flexible, adaptable structures of the Greater Vancouver Regional District would meet their criteria for "reinvented" government. It seems unlikely that they would be much interested in Ontario's long-standing debates about direct election to the upper tier or in solving coordination problems between the two tiers for certain functions by declaring one level or the other as sole authority. Indeed, official pronouncements in Ontario about local-government structures are still characterized by the rhetoric of a past era. Bigger is better; inter-municipal agreements are problems, not solutions; accountability to citizens can only be exercised through direct election. It is as though the academic theorists of public choice – and their recent popularizers, such as Osborne and Gaebler – simply do not exist.

The main value of the public-choice approach is that it forces us to confront new ways of structuring governmental arrangements, especially at the local level, so that governments become more responsive and efficient. Public choice harnesses the allocative strength of the marketplace to arrangements originally designed to respond only to the formal decisions of elected councils.

However, public choice may be of little use to provinces such as Ontario that are searching for new ways to make particular programs more equitable or fair. Followed to its ultimate conclusion, public choice makes it impossible for governments to bring about significant change: it is the marketplace – that is, efficiency rather than equity – that rules. In Canada, at least, this extreme is not politically defensible. That is why no provincial government concerned with equity is ever likely to let hundreds of municipal governments engage in cut-throat economic competition with one another.

What must be sought out is the middle ground between public choice and the traditional approach of the consolidationists. Among governments of Canada's city-regions, those of the GVRD seem to best represent what such a middle ground looks like in the real world. The GVRD is far from perfect. To be an effective decision-making institution for the entire city-region, its original land-use planning authority needs to be fully restored and perhaps even expanded. The fact that it has little or no involvement in public transit seems quite unjustified. There are perhaps ways in which its control over sewers and water-supply systems can be better integrated with the needs of the municipalities. But the GVRD does cover almost the entire city-region and its territory can easily be expanded. It is already involved in hospital planning and clearly has great potential as a locus for multi-functional planning for the whole area.

City-regions with single-tier comprehensive systems – Edmonton, Calgary, Winnipeg, London – need not be much concerned about bringing together all the area's municipal leaders to pursue common objectives. The city council serves the purpose well enough. From time to time, however, they will have to consider whether their respective areas need to be expanded still further, or perhaps (as was the case in Winnipeg) contracted. In these systems, the challenge is to exploit the virtues of comprehensiveness and direct political accountability, while avoiding the negative effects of monopoly and excessive size.

All other Canadian city-regions require an institution similar to the GVRD: one that is comprehensive in territory and flexible in function. Such institutions do not require large bureaucracies. In fact, they will probably work best if they have no operational responsibilities at all. Their aim should be to provide a forum where regional issues can be discussed, to act as a catalyst for the creation of inter-municipal agreements and special-purpose bodies and to enact planning documents with sufficient legal status to coerce municipalities into adhering to broad strategic objectives for the use of land. Inevitably, one of the central concerns of such an institution would be the state of the economy of the whole city-region. At a minimum, the regional institution would collect economic data and provide information. In some circumstances – such as in Montreal, perhaps – the need could be much more substantial: it could be called upon to prepare, in cooperation with other levels of government, a comprehensive plan for economic renewal.

Much more so than Americans, Canadians have been quick to adopt institutional change as a solution for urban problems. The Municipality of Metropolitan Toronto and Unicity in Winnipeg have been institutional innovations that have quite properly attracted attention throughout the industrialized world. The basic idea was to establish a new government for an entire city-region. But the days of creating new governments are over. As a way of solving urban problems, such a response is too costly, too inflexible and too disruptive of democratic local decision making.

Canadians too often forget that our provinces – whatever national or economic aspirations they claim to represent – are also simply the middle tier of a complex federal-provincial-municipal system. Within their respective territories, each includes a relatively small number of cities and their immediate hinterlands. Provinces act as the kind of large-scale regional governments that a good many countries are trying to invent. In an ideal world, some would draw our provincial boundaries differently. But, in reality, we know they are not going to change.

Our city-regions will never become provinces on their own, nor will their reorganized governmental structures ever be granted as much legal authority as the provincial legislatures that might create them. In these circumstances, the current challenge in Canada is to create institutional frameworks for city-regions in which inter-municipal decisions can be made and services arranged. The framework would not itself be a distinct level of government. Its purpose would be to enhance the capacity of provincial and municipal leaders to serve the needs of the people who elected them.

Notes

1. For a comprehensive survey of recent developments, see Allan O'Brien, *Municipal Consolidation in Canada and its Alternatives* (Toronto: ICURR Publications, 1993).

2. David Osborne and Ted Gaebler, *Reinventing Government* (New York: Penguin Books, 1993), p. 247.

Note on
Contributors

Andrew Sancton is a Professor of Political Science and Director of the Local Government Program at the University of Western Ontario. He is the author of *Governing the Island of Montreal: Language Differences and Metropolitan Politics* (Berkeley, CA: University of California Press, 1985). He has co-edited two collections of original essays: *City Politics in Canada*, with Warren Magnusson (Toronto: University of Toronto Press, 1983) and *Metropolitan Governance: American/Canadian Intergovernmental Perspectives*, with Donald N. Rothblatt (IGS Press at the University of California, 1993). He serves on the editorial board of *Canadian Public Administration* and the board of directors of the Ontario Municipal Management Institute. In the early 1980s, and again in the 1990s, he was a member of the federal Electoral Boundaries Commission for Ontario.

France St-Hilaire is a Research Director at IRPP and responsible for the City-Regions program. She has researched and written on Canadian public policy, economic development and tax policy. She has previously worked as a researcher at the University of Western Ontario and the University of Toronto and as an economic consultant. She is also the author of *Canadian High-Tech in a New World Economy: A Case Study of Information Technology* (with David W. Conklin, IRPP, 1988) and *Toward Sustainable Federalism: Reforming Federal-Provincial Fiscal Arrangements* (with Paul A.R. Hobson, IRPP, 1993).

Other publications in this series:

William J. Coffey, *The Evolution of Canada's Metropolitan Economies*

Recent IRPP publications

Public Finance

Paul A.R. Hobson and France St-Hilaire, *Toward Sustainable Federalism: Reforming Federal-Provincial Fiscal Arrangements*

Social Policy

Jean-Michel Cousineau, *La Pauvreté et l'État: Pour un nouveau partage des compétences en matière de sécurité sociale*

Ross Finnie, *Child Support: The Guideline Options*

Elisabeth B. Reynolds (ed.), *Income Security: Changing Needs, Changing Means*

Education

Edwin G. West, *Ending the Squeeze on Universities*

Peter Coleman, *Learning About Schools: What Parents Need to Know and How They Can Find Out*

Bruce Wilkinson, *Educational Choice: Necessary But Not Sufficient*

Governance

F. Leslie Seidle (ed.), *Rethinking Government: Reform or Reinvention?*

F. Leslie Seidle (ed.), *Equity and Community: The Charter, Interest Advocacy and Representation*

These and other IRPP publications are available from

Renouf Publishing
1294 Algoma Road
Ottawa, Ontario
K1B 3W8

Tel.: (613) 741-4333
Fax.: (613) 741-5439